Defining Hybrid Heroes

Defining Hybrid Heroes

The Leadership Spectrum from Scoundrel to Saint

Inge Brokerhof, Stephan Sonnenburg, and Greg Stone

ANTHEM PRESS

Anthem Press
An imprint of Wimbledon Publishing Company
www.anthempress.com

This edition first published in UK and USA 2024
by ANTHEM PRESS
75–76 Blackfriars Road, London SE1 8HA, UK
or PO Box 9779, London SW19 7ZG, UK
and
244 Madison Ave #116, New York, NY 10016, USA

British Library Cataloguing-in-Publication Data
A catalogue record for this book is available from the British Library.

Library of Congress Cataloging-in-Publication Data: 2024930954
A catalog record for this book has been requested.

ISBN-13: 978-1-83999-289-6 (Pbk)
ISBN-10: 1-83999-289-1 (Pbk)

This title is also available as an e-book.

CONTENTS

PROLOGUE

We decided to write this book for two reasons: (1) as far as we are able to determine, little has been written about hybrid heroes and (2) our insights emanate directly from the work we have done. The three of us started our collaboration with a stream of presentations at *The Art of Management & Organization Conference* in Brighton, United Kingdom, in September 2018. Though we had Skyped and emailed many times, we did not meet in person until the beginning of the event. As we shared a meal in an outdoor courtyard at a restaurant on a back street, our intellectual bond transformed instantly into friendship.

Inge Brokerhof (PhD) is an organizational psychologist, writer, trainer, and researcher at the Vrije Universiteit Amsterdam. In her research, she explores how stories influence career identity, future work selves and moral development and she has worked at Harvard Business School and the University of Bath. For her company, stories-@-work, she offers workshops, presentations, and university lectures about change rhetoric, storytelling, organizational psychology, and business ethics. She has also published short stories, poems, and songs.

Stephan Sonnenburg (Dr.) is a professor of branding, creativity, and innovation management at ICN Business School Paris-Nancy-Berlin. Before his academic career, he worked at advertising agencies and founded a management consulting firm focusing on the power of narratives in digital transformation. He is fond of saying that there is nothing as practical as a good theory, and that principle informs much of what we are trying to accomplish here.

Greg Stone is, in a sense, the "odd man out" as he is the only non-academic. He's an independent communications consultant and author. He has written two business books, one focusing on the power of the villain in storytelling, as well as a new mystery novel called *Dangerous Inspiration*, profiling a collection of artists who run the spectrum from virtue to violence.

INTRODUCTION

Heroes and heroines are everywhere. They figure prominently in many modern popular songs performed by David Bowie, Alesso, and Måns Zelmerlöw, who have all released tunes called "heroes," and in series and movies revolving around superheroes like *The Flash*, *Arrow*, *Wonder Woman*, and *Spiderman*, who ultimately save the world or even the entire universe. As far back as *Gilgamesh*, regarded as the earliest surviving work of great literature, the main character is described as "the most glorious amongst heroes! [...] the most eminent among men!" (app. 2000 B.C., see Heidel 1949, 8). That complex epic, written in cuneiform, describes the journey of the king of Uruk, who was part god and part human (Abusch 2001). The universal concept of heroism pervades many cultures and time periods, vide the *Iliad*, the *Odyssey*, the *Bhagavad Gita*, and many biblical stories.

The word "hero" can be broadly defined as "a person admired for achievements and noble qualities" (Merriam Webster 2023). The roots are Latin and Greek and point toward demi-gods or superhumans with transcendent capabilities. For millennia, they have inspired and motivated us, as their stories carry "transrational" knowledge about mores and values, spirituality and wisdom, and their journeys teach us to be more empathetic and to consider new perspectives (Allison and Goethals 2014). When we hear, watch, or read a heroic story, we can experience it through the hero's eyes and achieve a psychological state of euphoria, a feeling of invincibility, and a strong motivation to better ourselves (Algoe and Haidt 2009).

Joseph Campbell (1904–1987), one of the most influential and innovative mythographers of the twentieth century, created a model for the quintessential story, which he called the hero's journey (Campbell 2008). The basic motif is a transformation from one state of being to another in search of the source of life energy. Campbell's foundational work was the starting point for interdisciplinary research focusing on heroes, heroism, and heroic leadership (Drysdale et al. 2014; Allison and Goethals 2014), as well as a strong impetus for postheroic research, which views leadership activities as collective rather than individual (Crevani et al. 2007; Ryömä 2020). Until now, however, heroes or heroic acts have been defined and described in a static way on a journey toward sainthood, enlightenment, strength, and so on. In line with this, empirical studies show that heroes are perceived as smart, charismatic, strong, resilient, selfless, caring, inspiring, and reliable (Allison and Goethals 2014). Therefore, the imaginary field of the hero is opposed to that of the villain (Gölz 2019). This single focus on the hero with outstanding personal traits is rather limited and often pushes heroes into the domain of clean-cut and rather "flat" characters.

Moreover, a one-dimensional approach fails to take into account the vicissitudes and parallel developments of a hero's life. It is important to note that, depending on time and place, a hero can be regarded *simultaneously* as a saint, a scoundrel, or a fool. An example is the popular book and television series about Dexter Morgan, who can best be described as a murderer and a savior since he uses his unstoppable urge to kill to rid the street of dangerous criminals. But would you want a Dexter in your neighborhood (Amper 2010)? Does it make sense to empathize with him, and would that be dangerous? Indeed, the lines between saints, villains, fools, and victims have become blurred, and the modern hero displays a bundle of imperfections.

These indistinct boundaries may be the effect of an increasingly complex and global world, what Bauman (2011) calls a "liquid" society, with little security or certainty. People often assume that heroes are perfect in every aspect of their lives. But how do we evaluate the dedicated doctor who saves lives at work but neglects his family at home? Or the president who saves his country from a nuclear disaster and cheats regularly on his wife? Or the genius musician who abuses minors? Do saint-like heroes no longer exist? And how is this belief reflected in our culture and society?

Overview

In this book, we will approach the hero (and her or his journey) from a hybrid perspective, exploring the spectrum from scoundrel to saint. We will utilize a more dynamic, fluid, situational, and performative outlook than in heroism science (Allison and Goethals 2014), postheroism studies (Crevani et al. 2007), or research in the interplay between heroic and postheroic leadership (Ryömä 2020), which approach heroic or postheroic phenomena more in a black-and-white and mainly a good-versus-evil way of thinking. We will examine the field from several distinct points of view, through lenses dominated by fiction, business, politics, and psychology, as we paint a new, more complex portrait that resonates with the complexities of modern-day reality. While each chapter adopts a unique perspective, all of the chapters build logically on each other, starting with a theoretical introduction to hybrid heroes, followed by a conceptual framework for hybrid heroes, and concluding with case studies.

In Chapter 1, "The Role of Hybrid Heroes in Popular Stories and in Moral Leadership," Inge Brokerhof shows how charming rogues in popular culture can influence career identity and complicate the drive toward moral leadership. For instance, the appeal of charismatic but morally ambiguous characters like Jordan Belford in *The Wolf of Wall Street* or Harvey Specter from *Suits* can subvert the moral compass of young executives when values are ambiguous, situational, and contextual. The influence of hybrid heroes and their stories on career identity is theorized to occur via three different pathways, each shaping identity in a distinct way. Furthermore, this chapter will explore the link between moral leadership and hybrid heroes. The rise of hybrid perceptions of heroism in turbulent times of change can polarize instead of unite. What are the consequences and dangers of revering hybrid heroes? Surprisingly, their complexity can also inspire us and even spur moral development when critical reflection is prompted by these complex role models.

In Chapter 2, "Isn't Every Heroic Person on a Hybrid Journey? Joseph Campbell Revisited," Stephan Sonnenburg elaborates on the model of the hero's journey, a generic motif about finding a way to transform the social world into a richer condition. Although the hero's journey is a powerful metaphor, there are some flaws in the framework. It has focused mostly on men on the move, but not women, teams, or other social constellations. In addition, the journey centers on a sequential series of setbacks, fears, woes, and stuttering progress in the transformation from benevolence to evil. To tackle these issues, the hybrid heroic journey is instead a new framework combining insights from the classical hero's journey with selected cards from a system of archetypes and the major arcana of tarot.

In Chapter 3, "Hybrid Heroes in Extremis and at Work," Greg Stone surveys the roles that heroes, villains, sages, and fools play in commerce, with illustrative tales of famous rebels and unorthodox but successful entrepreneurs. We will also meet a bank robber with a Harvard degree and a murderer who became a law professor. Moreover, Greg outlines the long tradition of fools in literature, notably *King Lear*'s jester, *Henry IV*'s Falstaff, and *Of Mice and Men*'s Lenny, to name a few.

The overall lessons to be gleaned from our work on hybrid heroes are that perfection is elusive (if it exists at all) and that the prevailing image of an ideal heroic leader who is noble, honorable, who makes the morally "right" decisions, works long hours, controls his emotions and never shows weakness (Binns 2008, 601) is an illusion. Our worship of heroes represents a romantic longing (Goethals and Alison 2019), which often makes us "overlook" their dark sides or even villainy. Yet, the scoundrel often goes hand in hand with the saint. For example, the most effective hybrid heroes are often capable of great compassion and ruthlessness at the same time. Shedding light on the hybridity of our heroes and heroic leaders can be liberating. It can deepen our understanding of the organizational, cultural, and societal values that underlie heroism, and inspire us during our own personal journeys, enhancing the way we understand ourselves. In complex times, wherein heroes become hybrid and perceived certainties crumble, a more complex and ambiguous notion of heroism offers us new modes of understanding leadership.

According to Campbell (2003), heroes sometimes ride "on the great rhythm of the historical process" (57), like Napoleon who made this startling statement at the beginning of his Russia campaign: "I feel myself driven towards an end that I do not know. As soon as I shall have reached it, as soon as I shall become unnecessary, an atom will suffice to shatter me. Till then, not all the forces of mankind can do anything against me" (Campbell 2003, 57). We hope to explore that wondrous intricacy as we take a journey together through the hero's skewed and paradoxical perspective. Perhaps the last word belongs to Tywin Lannister from George R. R. Martin's *Game of Thrones*: "The greatest of fools are at times more clever than the men who laugh at them" ("Storm of Swords" episode).

References

Abusch, Tzvi. 2001. The Development and Meaning of the Epic of Gilgamesh: An Interpretive Essay. *Journal of the American Oriental Society* 121, no. 4: 614–622.

Algoe, Sara B. and Haidt, Jonathan. 2009. Witnessing Excellence in Action: The 'Other–Praising' Emotions of Elevation, Gratitude, and Admiration. *The Journal of Positive Psychology* 4, no. 2: 105–127.

Allison, Scott T. and Goethals, George R. 2014. "Now He Belongs to the Ages": The Heroic Leadership Dynamic and Deep Narratives of Greatness. In *Conceptions of Leadership: Enduring Ideas and Emerging Insights*, edited by George R. Goethals, Scott T. Allison, Roderick M. Kramer and David M. Messick, 167–183. New York: Palgrave Macmillan.

Amper, Susan. 2010. Dexter's Dark World: The Serial Killer as Superhero. In *Serial Killers – Philosophy for Everyone: Being and Killing*, edited by Signe Waller, 3–113. West Sussex: Wiley–Blackwell.

Bauman, Zygmunt. 2011. *Liquid Modernity*. Cambridge: Polity Press.

Binns, Jennifer. 2008. The Ethics of Relational Leading: Gender Matters. *Gender, Work & Organization* 15, no. 3: 600–620.

Bowie, David. 1977. *Heroes: On Heroes (Record)*. New York: RCA Records.

Campbell, Jospeh. 2008. *The Hero's Journey: Joseph Campbell on his Life and Work*. Novato: New World Library.

———. 2008. *The Hero with a Thousand Faces (3rd Edition)*. Novato: New World Library.

Crevani, Lucia, Lindgren, Monica and Packendorff, Johann. 2007. Shared Leadership: A Postheroic Perspective on Leadership as a Collective Construction. *International Journal of Leadership Studies* 3, no. 1: 40–67.

Drysdale, Lawrie, Bennett, Jeffrey, Murakami, Elizabeth T., Johansson, Olaf and
Gurr, David. 2014. Heroic Leadership in Australia, Sweden, and the United States.
International Journal of Educational Management 28, no. 7: 785–797.

Goethals, George R. and Allison, Scott T. 2019. *The Romance of Heroism and Heroic
Leadership.* Bingley: Emerald Publishing Limited.

Gölz, Olmo. 2019. The Imaginary Field of the Heroic: On the Contention between
Heroes, Martyrs, Victims and Villains in Collective Memory. *helden. heroes. héros.:
E-Journal on Cultures of the Heroic,* special issue 5: 27–38.

Heidel, Alexander. 1949. *Gilgamesh Epic and Old Testament Parallels (Volume 136).* Chicago:
University of Chicago Press.

Merriam Webster. 2023. Hero. 11 July. https://www.merriam-webster.com/dictionary/
hero.

Ryömä, Arto. 2020. The Interplay of Heroic and Post-heroic Leadership: Exploring
Tensions in Leadership Manifestations in the Oscillations between Onstage and
Offstage Contexts. *Scandinavian Journal of Management* 36, no. 1: 1–15.

Chapter 1

THE ROLE OF HYBRID HEROES IN POPULAR STORIES AND MORAL LEADERSHIP

By Inge Brokerhof

"We are the heroes of our time
But we're dancing with the demons in our minds."

Zelmerlöw (2015)

Winning song at the 2015 Eurovision Song Contest

This chapter will zoom in on the villain-hero dynamic in fictional narratives and its impact on career identity and conceptualizations of moral leadership in business contexts. Illustrated by empirical research, I will describe how hybrid heroes and their journeys can influence career identity via different pathways. Second, I will explore the influence of the hybrid hero on the field of leadership—presenting a more dynamic perspective on leaders in the context of situational and temporal change. A link between heroic leadership and hybrid heroes will be theorized. Can we be the saint-like heroes we often initially aspire to become? A more complex and holistic perception of heroism may broaden our understanding of moral leadership. Moreover, the hybrid hero spectrum could offer people a window into the morally ambiguous parts within themselves, stimulating conscious, critical reflection.

In my chapter, I consciously use the term "hero" to refer to *all* genders. This is partly because I am not keen on the word "heroine" to specifically refer to female heroes, and also because the traditional male connotation feels outdated. Everyone can be a hero.

Villain-Heroes in Fictional Narratives and Literature

"I'm a very neat monster.
How many more bodies would there have been had I not gotten to
those killers? I didn't want to save lives, but save lives I did."

Dexter Morgan
(Lindsay 2004)

Jeff Lindsay's books featuring Dexter Morgan tell the story of a man with a troubled childhood who grows up to be a hero and a villain at the same time. Early on, his adoptive father realizes that Dexter has psychopathic traits that fit early onset conduct disorder (formerly labeled "psychopathy") with an insuppressible urge to kill. His father teaches him to at least follow a strict moral code when he kills, and he becomes a dark vigilante. During the day, Dexter works as a blood spatter analyst for the police, yet at night he kills rapists and murderers who are slipping through the cracks of the legal system. This makes him both villain and saint—a morally ambiguous hybrid hero (Amper 2010; Brophy 2010; Van Tourhout 2019). This leads to troubling questions: Should we worry if a serial killer like Dexter lives in our neighborhood? Should we rely solely on law enforcement for safekeeping? Or would we secretly want a Dexter to protect us? When we sympathize with him, we likely feel empathy for him and might even value his murderous behavior (Brophy 2010).

Dexter's story illustrates a new conception and expansion of the heroism spectrum. While in the past, heroes were always essentially *good,* their modern counterparts are flawed in many ways—including even intentional villainy. The onset of the twenty-first century has shown an increase of this type of hybrid hero—the villain-hero—in popular culture, such as John Smith (*The Man in the High Castle*), Harvey Specter (*Suits*), Beth Boland (*Good Girls*), Tokyo (*La Casa De Papel/ Money Heist*) and Francis Underwood (*House of Cards*) (see Table 1.1). Their moral duality has blurred perceptions of good and bad, where the good is never fully good and the bad never fully bad. The villain-hero has saint-like characteristics associated with "classic" heroes, such as nobility, moral leadership, selflessness, sacrifice, and a willingness to fight for the common good (Sullivan and Venter 2010), but at the same time might be egotistic, immoral, violent, or murderous, with poor impulse and/or emotional control (Martin Del Campo 2017).

In traditional (fairy) tales, villains challenge heroes and spur them on to superhuman deeds. After the dragon has been slain, the monster beheaded, or the murderer locked up in prison, the hero returns home as a savior (Booker 2004). Yet, in the past decades, morally ambiguous protagonists in popular

Table 1.1 Examples of hybrid heroes in popular fiction.

Hybrid Hero Character	Short Description	Novel, Movie or TV Series
Dexter Morgan	A blood spatter analyst for the FBI by day and vigilante at night, who takes out his innate psychopathic urges to kill murderers who escaped the justice system.	Jeff Lindsay's novel *Darkly Dreaming Dexter (2004)* and TV series (2006–2013)
John Smith	In an alternative reality, Hitler and the Nazis have won World War II. Smith, a former U.S. Army captain, has joined the "Schutzstaffel" (SS) following the surrender of the United States and becomes a Reichsführer, who is loyal to Nazi ideology but also displays heroism.	TV series *The Man in the High Castle* (2015–2019) based on the by novel by Philip K. Dick (1962).
Harvey Specter	A successful senior partner at a prestigious law firm in New York, who is portrayed as a morally ambiguous hero.	TV series *Suits* (2011–2019)
Beth Boland	A suburban mother of four, who encounters financial problems after her husband cheats on her and leaves her penniless. She robs a supermarket and gets increasingly drawn into a career as a professional criminal.	TV series *Good Girls* (2018–2021)
Tokyo	A rebellious yet passionate bank robber, who with a team of seven chosen bank robbers, ingeniously robs the Royal Mint in Madrid.	TV series *La Casa de Papel (Money Heist)* (2017–2021)
Francis Underwood	A ruthless American politician who rises in the U.S. government through dirty tactics such as duplicity, deception, and even murder.	TV series *House of Cards* (2013–2018)
Anna Sorokin	A Russian-born woman who infiltrates New York's high society under the fake identity of Anna Delvey, a German socialite and heiress to a fortune. She schemes and scams her new friends out of millions.	TV mini-series *Inventing Anna* (2022)

books, plays, and movies have been slowly on the rise, including multilayered villains (Martin Del Campo 2017). Still, the pervasive presence of the *fully blended* villain-hero can be considered a new phenomenon, starting in the beginning of the twenty-first century (Van Tourhout 2019). Contrary to the anti-hero—who has some personal flaws but ultimately strives for the "good" and will save the world anyway (e.g., Character Carrie Mathison in *Homeland* who struggles with mental illness, or *Shrek,* an ogre who becomes a non-ste-reotypical hero against his will)—the villain-hero actively and purposefully engages in villainous acts. Also, tales do not end on a happy or "morally pure" note. The journey of the villain-hero thereby also deviates from the classical hero's journey as described by Joseph Campbell (1949; more in Chapter 2).

Of course, no work of art is created in a vacuum, and therefore hybrid heroes at large, and villain-heroes in particular, are a direct reflection of a changing world. They can therefore be interpreted as a response to increased moral complexity caused by the current era of "liquid modernity," character-ized by neoliberalism, uncertainty, privatization, blurred societal boundaries, individualism, and the information revolution (Bauman 2013). Moreover, high-impact events such as 9/11 may have sparked the conception of villain-heroes (Van Tourhout 2019), along with recent crises such as COVID-19. Cinelli and colleagues (2020) found that amidst the chaos of the pandemic, information from questionable news sources spread in the same fashion on social media just as rapidly as information from reliable news sources, creat-ing an "infodemic" that led to great confusion. This misinformation may have blurred the distinctions between "good" and "bad," and even more so between heroes and villains.

The "moral" in popular stories reflects this ambiguity, creating fertile ground for the villain-hero. In addition, the lockdowns imposed by govern-ments during the pandemic may have sparked interest in characters defying the current social and political system, like Tokyo in *La Casa De Papel* or Anna in the mini-series *Inventing Anna* (see Table 1.1). While these characters rob banks and cheat people out of their money, viewers nonetheless empathize with them and admire them. Ultimately, art imitates life and life imitates art. Through the production *and* consumption of narrative—whether through lit-erature, movies, or online streaming series—we cope with both personal as well as societal change. We create hybrid heroes in stories who, at the same time, influence us, contributing to a continuous vicious cycle of personal and sociocultural change.

How Hybrid Heroes in Fiction Can Influence (Career) Identity

"Instead of calling them role models, I call them heroes. I think if you tell me who your heroes are, I can tell you how you're gonna turn out to quite an extent."

Warren Buffett (1998)
(Investor Archive 2020)

People need heroes to look up to. In fact, they are even motivated to create them—especially in times of uncertainty and change. In their book on heroic leadership, Goethals and Allison (2019) note that when people are asked about their heroes, they often give examples of fictional characters. Indeed, fictional narratives can influence our sense of self, including our career identity and aspirations for the future (Brokerhof et al. 2018). Stories in novels, movies, and television series can help us to define ourselves in relation to our work, inspire us to think about who we aspire to become in our future career, and encourage us to reflect on our moral character in the workplace and what type of employee or employer we want to be (Brokerhof 2021).

Stories can serve as mirrors. By understanding different characters, we become more competent in understanding other people (Kidd and Castano 2013) and ultimately ourselves (Slater et al. 2014). We temporarily see the world through the characters' eyes, and—even when they are doing morally questionable things—we start to root for them. For example, we might fervently hope that serial killer Dexter will not get caught by the police. The playful nature of stories gives us license to suspend our (moral) judgment, a phenomenon referred to as *the willing suspension of disbelief* (Ferri 2007). Suspending our moral judgment can help us experience the story on a deeper level because we can allow ourselves to be uncritically absorbed into the tale, a mental process referred to as narrative transportation (Busselle and Bilandzic 2009). Indeed, research has shown that in stories with morally ambiguous characters, we hold in check our judgment and our self-regulatory mechanisms that separate right from wrong (Bandura 2002) in order to facilitate enjoyment (Zillmann 1988).

The experience of becoming absorbed into a narrative world and identifying with its main character can change us, because part of the character and the story (temporarily) resides in who we are. Slater and colleagues (2014) theorize that the mechanism behind this change is a process they call *expanding the boundaries of self*: when we are absorbed into a story, we are temporarily relieved from regulating our self-concept, and we can explore new identities and perspectives. Moreover, the playful character of stories can induce identity play—the almost flirtatious processes we engage in while exploring new possible future selves (Ibarra and Petriglieri 2010) as we temporarily merge with fictional characters (Oatley 1999). This process is likely to influence our identity and our moral judgment. While the moral disengagement promoted by the willing suspension of disbelief might be temporary, it could become a pervasive part of our self, changing who we are or influencing who we want to become in the future (Brokerhof 2021).

Stories and story characters can influence or shape our identity in the context of work (Brokerhof 2021). Modern careers are not tied to one specific job and extend beyond organizations (Arthur et al. 2016). Instead, they have become boundaryless—encompassing several work roles, companies, and functions (Arthur et al. 2016). Since our career identity can function as a compass to navigate work-related decisions, a well-developed career identity narrative is regarded as advantageous for our development (Fugate et al. 2004). Stories help to construct our narrative identity in general (McAdams 2008) and our career identity in particular (Meijers 1998). They can inspire sustainable employability—stimulating people to adopt a long-term vision toward their careers (Brokerhof et al. 2020). In my previous research, I have identified three different pathways through which fictional narratives can stimulate identity change: the personal, the narrative, and the reflective pathway (Brokerhof et al. 2018; Brokerhof 2020). Figure 1.1 shows how these different types of hybrid hero narratives could affect our career identity.

This model approaches identity from a dialogical perspective, conceptualizing the self as a cacophony of different voices that are in constant communication with one another (Hermans 2014). These voices—or *I-positions*—encompass character traits, roles, goals, role models and possible future (work) selves and they sometimes align and sometimes conflict. For example, they may encompass opposing traits such as "me as ambitious" and "me as lazy," or at certain moments, possibly conflicting goals such as "me as a devoted mother" versus "me as a careerwoman." When they are in conflict, we need to negotiate between different I-positions. Narrative structures can help us to create a coherent perception of self. Together all these different

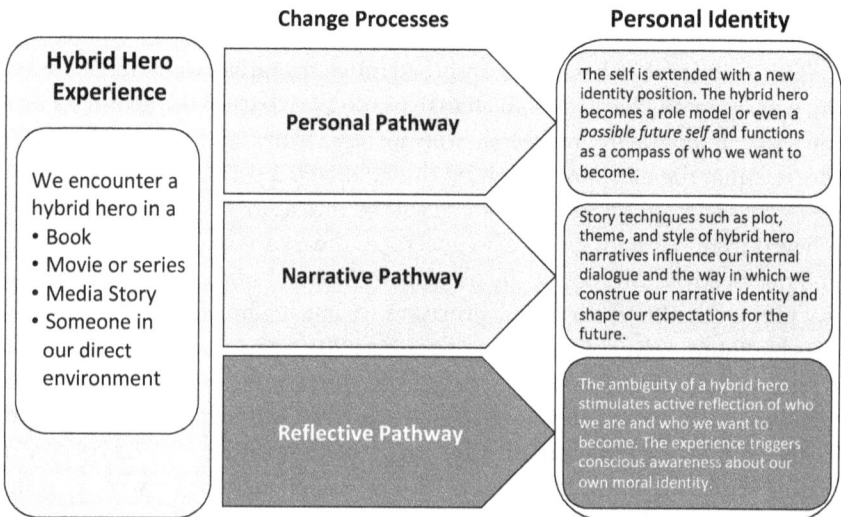

Change Processes		Personal Identity
Hybrid Hero Experience		
We encounter a hybrid hero in a • Book • Movie or series • Media Story • Someone in our direct environment	**Personal Pathway**	The self is extended with a new identity position. The hybrid hero becomes a role model or even a *possible future self* and functions as a compass of who we want to become.
	Narrative Pathway	Story techniques such as plot, theme, and style of hybrid hero narratives influence our internal dialogue and the way in which we construe our narrative identity and shape our expectations for the future.
	Reflective Pathway	The ambiguity of a hybrid hero stimulates active reflection of who we are and who we want to become. The experience triggers conscious awareness about our own moral identity.

Figure 1.1 Process model of identity change instigated by hybrid heroes. Adapted from Brokerhof et al. (2018) and Brokerhof (2020, 2021).

selves, and our internal dialogue that builds bridges between them, define who we are. We apply dialogical selves theory to career identity and define this as "the interactive structure of I-positions comprising a person's self-definition in the context of work and career, which guides career aspirations, motivations and behavior" (Brokerhof 2021, 12).

Via the personal pathway, hybrid hero characters can influence us when they become role models (Gibson 2004) or *possible future (work) selves*—who we aspire to become in our personal future (Markus and Nurius 1986) or future career (Strauss et al. 2012), either consciously or subconsciously. Thus, we *add* another I-position to our internal dialogue. People may emulate their favorite (fictional) characters—including villain-heroes—without conscious, critical reflection. In an interview study, my colleagues and I found, for example, many students who aspired to become Harvey Specter in *Suits* or Jordan Belfort from *The Wolf of Wall Street* (Brokerhof 2021). Interestingly, the prominence of these characters with stereotypical "masculine" attributes, appears to signify (possibly subconscious) gendered notions of heroic business leaders (Fletcher 2004). The influences of hybrid heroes could be subtle—that is, adopting a character trait or a certain lifestyle—or they could go as far as complete imitation. The character of Dexter Morgan has actually inspired people to commit murder exactly in his style. For instance, the aspiring filmmaker Mark Twitchell, a great admirer of Dexter, admitted to murdering someone in Dexter mode and was sentenced to prison for life (CBC 2011).

In the narrative pathway, devices such as plot, style, theme, or metaphors often subconsciously become templates that help shape our internal dialog and determine *how* we balance our different and, at times, competing identity positions (selves, roles, goals, and character traits). They may lead us to ask: What part of me will be most prominent in the current context? Additionally, these devices are the materials we use to construct our narrative identity, that is, the story of who we are, which creates continuity in how we experience ourselves (McAdams 2008). The plotlines, themes, and style of the hybrid hero's journey in stories thereby also influence us. While in classic hero narratives the good will ultimately prevail, in hybrid hero tales, the story is more morally complex. Evil may prevail, the villain-hero may spin out of control, s/he may win at great cost to society, or s/he may simply become a monster. Since the narrative elements we experience in our culture (sometimes without conscious awareness) inspire our own narrative identity (McAdams 2008), hybrid hero stories could shape our expectations for the future and might make us cynical or make immoral behavior seem "normal."

The reflective pathway of narrative influence shows how we can be influenced by hybrid hero stories when they make us aware of and consciously reflect on the moral ambiguity of their characters. Reflection often happens when a story somehow disturbs us to such an extent that we feel the need to think about it in more depth, generating deliberate, conscious reflection (Kahneman and Frederick 2005). People have a tendency for quick, dichotomous thinking—that is, "all" or "nothing" and "good" or "bad" (Oshio 2012). Reflection on hybrid hero stories could counteract this binary way of thinking and help people to grasp the ethical complexity and the moral messiness of real life. Thus, villain-hero narratives could spark discussions about moral complexity in our culture and society and may even offer us a window into morally ambiguous characteristics within ourselves, stimulating conscious, critical reflection.

When it comes to career decisions, hybrid hero narratives could influence the direction people take in their working lives via these three pathways (Brokerhof 2021). For example, my colleagues and I studied the influence of the story of *The Wolf of Wall Street* on business school students and sales professionals (Brokerhof 2021). This story revolves around the career of Jordan Belfort, a successful yet corrupt sales professional who enriches himself by selling worthless penny stocks to ignorant buyers. A Hollywood movie based on his book (2011) depicts the extensive wealth, decadent parties, and culture of rampant greed on Wall Street without overt criticism (Salek 2018). We found that the character of Belfort appealed to business students' and sales professionals' desired future work selves—who they aspire to become in their future careers (Strauss et al. 2012). His persona was perceived through the "winner frame" of a self-made hero. This winner frame was related to subsequent lower empathy levels compared to a narrative of victims of financial malpractice (Brokerhof 2021). Presented as a hero in the Hollywood movie, Belfort, played by the famous actor Leonardo DiCaprio, ultimately gets away with everything he has done despite his corruption and clearly villainous behavior. As the movie attracted a large audience, this hybrid hero narrative has the potential to influence many people's career aspirations. Thus, the story of *The Wolf of Wall Street* might represent a culture of greed, but it could also perpetuate this culture (for details, see Brokerhof 2021).

In my research on the influence of narrative fiction on people's career identity, future work selves, and moral development, morally ambiguous fictional characters, such as Jordan Belfort and Harvey Specter (see Table 1.1), often popped up as career role models (Brokerhof 2021). The way in which participants talked about those characters indicated they had become an I-position in the career identity of participants via the personal pathway in Figure 1.1 (Brokerhof 2021). While it is hard to assess the pervasiveness and longevity of this influence, it parallels the influence of Oliver Stone's movie *Wall Street*, released in 1987, which depicted the destructive effects of financial greed. Similar to "art for activism" movements, it was meant to raise awareness and make the viewer reflect on the culture of cupidity on Wall Street (Arsenault 1998). However, contrary to its intentions, the film became a cult phenomenon, whereby students imitated the dress, hairstyle—and ultimately—the attitude of the main character (Guerrera 2010). While Stone may have wanted to stimulate reflection (via the reflective pathway in the hybrid hero model in Figure 1), the movie more likely stimulated people via the personal pathway, whereby they imitated the main character with little critical consideration.

There are indications that telling a hybrid hero story from the perspective of the victims of the hybrid hero could invoke more conscious, critical deliberation, activating the reflective pathway (Brokerhof 2021). Furthermore, it is plausible that group discussions could shed a different light on hybrid hero narratives, broadening people's perspectives and sparking more conscious and critical reflection. In the last part of this chapter, we will zoom in on this particular use of narrative fiction in the context of business ethics education and what it may mean for hybrid hero tales.

Temporal Hybridity of Heroes and Leaders

"When heroes fall from the sky, many more will learn to fly."

Tony Meloto (n.d.)
(AZQuotes.com 2024)

Heroism and leadership can be considered closely intertwined. Heroes and leaders are exemplary and charismatic people who can motivate followers toward a common goal (Goethals and Allison 2019). Leadership has often been studied through the lens of heroism, with the leader at the glorious center of a success story (Ryömä 2020). This dominant conceptualization has also evoked a countermovement during the past two decades labeled "post-heroic leadership," which opposes this "domination of heroic figures and their great stories" (Ryömä 2020, 2) and instead emphasizes non-authoritarian, supportive, and "less individualistic, more relational" (Fletcher 2004, 648) attributes of leadership. While there has been a shift in dominant notions of what "good" leadership should entail—whereby a good leader is supportive, relationship-oriented, or even a servant to those who s/he leads, as in the servant leadership concept (Parris et al. 2013), still a strong focus remains on personality-based trait-like notions of leadership (e.g., Brown and Treviño 2006). Thus, while desired leadership qualities may have shifted, the cult around the leader-as-person remains, especially in popular culture.

As leaders, hybrid heroes can impact not only individual identities but groups of people in society at large. At the same time, cultural or national heroes reflect what people consider to be exemplary deeds and honorable traits (Bröckling 2019). Thus, heroes are socially constructed. When perceptions of merit change, former heroes can become non-heroes or no-longer-heroes (Bröckling 2019). The iconoclasm blowing over the world during the equality protests in 2020 after the death of George Floyd illustrates a recent example of how heroes can literally fall from their pedestals: the statue of Columbus was beheaded (in Boston), statues of Ghandi (in Amsterdam) and Winston Churchill were branded as "racists" with graffiti, and a statue of Edward Colton was thrown into the water (in Bristol) (Brus et al. 2020). Additionally, during turbulent cultural change, the same person can be socially constructed as a hero as well as a villain. As Bröckling (2019) writes, "heroic narratives polarize: one can revere their protagonists or hate them; one can admire or laugh at them—but one cannot remain indifferent to them" (39). The simultaneous view of a leader as a hero as well as a villain is a phenomenon which can be labeled heroic hybridity in time. This hybridity can be a polarizing agent, but it also represents a window for change.

An often-described phenomenon is that victors write history (e.g., Carlson and Farrelly 2022). Thereby, they determine the dominant narrative (often preserved in history books, art, and statues) and who is portrayed as a hero. Propaganda thus can reframe violent conquerors as heroic peacemakers after they have gained power, erasing their villainous side and their initial hybridity. Consequently, statues or commemorations of heroes do not represent history but rather promote hegemonic ideology. However, as societies change, so do their heroes—and thereby, iconoclastic heroes-turned-villains have been a common phenomenon in the course of history (Gamboni 2013). When interpreted through the framework of Joseph Campbell (1949), the journey of the hybrid hero radically differs from the "traditional" (or idealized) hero's. In his famous work, Campbell described 17 stages through which a hero passes on an adventure into the unknown as s/he encounters a challenging crisis, transforms in the journey toward victory, and then triumphantly returns as a changed (wo)man. When we encounter hybridity, the reverse can happen: those formerly considered heroes can cross the threshold to become villains. As a result of societal change and awareness, followers might abandon or reject their former leader(s). This shows how fleeting perceived heroism can be and how much contextual, temporal, and cultural factors play a role in the process. These transformations largely involve changes in *public perception*. Indeed, Goethals and Allison (2019) emphasize that heroes are created merely in our minds. Those we regard as heroes on a societal level mark the norms, values, and accomplishments that we deem important at that particular moment. Heroes are therefore bound to time and space. This type of temporal heroic hybridity can spark a broader discussion about dominant ideology. For instance, the "successful" occupiers of the "new" land were revered by many people in Europe in colonial times, while now they are regarded as "hostile occupiers," engaging in villainous acts to reign over the original people. While the iconoclasm of colonial commemorations is sometimes perceived as ending in a stalemate between opposing social perceptions, it can also be seen as a pivotal mark in the process of change (Carlson and Farrelly 2022). As Carlson and Farrelly (2022) state, "while our colonial commemorations supposedly reflect what we as a society value, so too does our protest against these commemorations" (16) and "whether the statues are toppled, rectified, or left alone is less important than the ongoing discussion they inspire about what we choose to remember and who we are today" (19).

In the digital era, new perspectives toward heroism are often only one computer click away, yet this abundance of varied opinions does not necessarily increase openness toward new modes of thinking. Social media could actually make people more close-minded via mechanisms that function as "echo chambers," special algorithms designed to attract attention, which expose people continuously to their own worldviews (Cinelli et al. 2021). At the same time, the information revolution and digital era have spurred complexity and uncertainty (Bauman 2013), and, according to Goethals and Allison (2019), it is uncertainty that motivates people, often unconsciously, to seek heroes to help them make sense of ambiguities. Thus, in uncertain times, people may be extra motivated to have heroes, craving this categorization to create order in the chaos of life (Goethals and Allison 2019). The way people mentally classify leaders as "heroes" or "villains" often happens via implicit psychological processes such as scripts, heuristics, and intuitions (e.g., Sonneshein 2007; Mandler 2014). Once we have labeled someone a hero because we think this person represents nobility, personal sacrifice, and the selfless strive for the common good (Sullivan and Venter 2010), it can be hard to acknowledge her or his darker side. To preserve a firm sense of identity, different groups cling to their existing ideology, which gives them a feeling of stability and an anchor in an uncertain world. Due to confirmation bias, whereby people look for information that confirms their existing feelings and ideas (e.g., Wason 1968), people often become more confident in their categorizations. People *need* their heroes, and they often work hard to maintain their saint-like image (Goethals and Allison 2019). The widespread iconoclasm of 2020 did not happen overnight and involves a value-based societal change (Brus et al. 2020) demonstrating that dominant societal paradigms *can* shift. Yet, the transformation from heroes to villains may be painful, since heroic worship resembles a romantic longing (Goethals and Allison 2019). Changing perceptions of a hero means letting go of your admiration of a beloved figure, which takes time, effort, and courage.

Some heroes remain hybrid for a long time, loved by some (and perceived as heroes) while hated by others (and perceived as villains), whereby conflicting views coexist, polarizing people into opposing camps. Former president Donald Trump is a case in point (Goethals and Allison 2019). His controversial personality seems to push people in opposite evaluations, particularly into "hero frames" *and* "villain frames" at the same time. While this is, of course, common in history, modern information systems both highlight and stimulate this hybridity. Another example is Michael Jackson. Some fans worship him and his journey, but at the same time, several narratives of pedophilia have also pushed him—mostly postmortem—into the "villain" category. Many radio stations stopped playing his songs, almost as an audio-iconoclastic act. This raises indeed a difficult ethical question: can we still appreciate beautiful music even when it is made by someone who may have committed grave crimes? Perhaps some accept both stories simultaneously: the heroic black musician who revolutionized popular music *and* the conflicting narratives of his victims, who will suffer for the rest of their lives with the damage he has caused them. Others may simply deny or defy. It is, however, hard for either camp to ignore the hybridity of his *persona*.

Besides famous people like Donald Trump and Michael Jackson, cultural icons, present in folklore traditions, can also follow the journey of hybrid heroism. This can eventually be a fruitful foundation for cultural transformation. A Dutch example of this is the case of "Zwarte Piet"—"Black Pete," the iconic black helper in the traditional holiday of Sinterklaas (see Case 1). This case illustrates how slowly rising public awareness of the racist and colonial roots of a former admired, traditional icon, led to more than a decade of emotionally heated debate. Currently, the hybridity of this cultural icon can be regarded as a stage in the process of adaptive change, whereby the icon is adapting in response to the growing awareness of the Dutch colonial past. Temporal hybridity makes this change possible, allowing space in the public debate for various opinions, with mixed perceptions, reshaping cultural traditions so that an adjusted heroic icon might emerge (see Figure 2).

CASE 1. TEMPORAL HYBRIDITY IN THE PERCEPTION OF DUTCH CULTURAL ICON "BLACK PETE"

In mid-November, "Sinterklaas" (traditionally based on Saint Nicholas) arrives in the Netherlands with his helpers, all originally called "Black Pete" ("Zwarte Piet"). Children put their shoes next to the chimney, and during the night, the "Peters" climb down the chimney to put a small present inside the shoes. For decades, this tradition was so highly embedded in society that the image of "Black Pete" was fully institutionalized. In November and December, it was impossible to escape the character, who appeared in store windows, schools, and businesses. Adults often dressed up as "Black Pete" (with blackface) as part of a televised national parade. According to legend, Pete had dark skin because he was stained with chimney soot, but several other features (such as Afro wigs, full lips, golden hoop earrings, and clothing) reflected the image of the original people from the Dutch colonial past (McDonald–Gibson 2020).

Dutch immigrants of color began to question the tradition, and in 2011, the "Kick Out Zwarte Piet" movement came into being. It encountered a great deal of resistance. In 2014, even the Dutch prime minister, Mark Rutte, laughed at the issue and defended Black Pete as an innocent children's holiday (NOS 2014). The hybridity of Black Pete actually created a rift in society, dividing the Dutch into pro-Black Pete and anti-Black Pete movements. Millions of people signed online peti-tions ("pete-titions") to advocate that the character should stay (NOS 2013), and the first anti-Black Pete protesters encountered verbal and physical violence (McDonald–Gibson 2020). Over more than a decade after the worldwide Black Lives Matter protests in 2020, the movement suddenly received a boost in public support. In fact, while in 2019, 71 percent of the Dutch wanted to maintain the traditional appearance of Pete, this figure dropped to 47 percent in 2020 (McDonald–Gibson 2020). In addition, online platforms, such as Instagram, Google, and Facebook decided to ban images of Black Pete. While we are writing this book, the change is still in process, but the name "Pete" is used now with a new image—representing people of all skin colors with black "chimney" smudges. In the spring of 2022, a local political party called "Zwarte Piet is Zwart" (Black Pete is Black) campaigned for office in of the one of the bigger towns in the Netherlands, but they did not receive enough votes to get elected.

While the example of Pete refers to a hybrid icon resembling that of a fictional character—who *can* be transformed—not all temporally hybrid heroes can withstand cultural change, nor should they. At a personal level, as described above, hybrid heroes could offer people the opportunity to reflect on the morally ambiguous or shadow side of themselves, and at the level of society, hybrid heroes could expose moral obscurities, shared trauma, and ethical double standards embedded in society. Thus, some former heroes become non-heroes or no-longer-heroes (Bröckling 2019) when they are de-heroized.

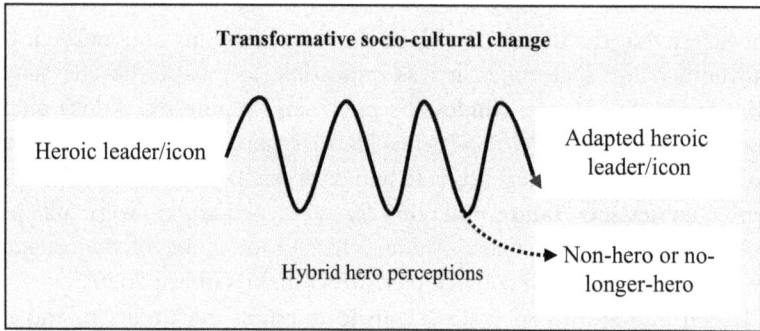

Figure 1.2 Temporal hybridity in the process of sociocultural change.

They will not be remembered as heroes—or they will not be remembered at all (Figure 1.2).

The Link between Hybrid Heroes and Moral Leadership

"Perhaps those who are best suited to power are those who have never sought it."

Albus Dumbledore in Harry Potter and the Deathly Hallows
(Rowling 2013)

Classical heroes are often considered "highly moral," selflessly dedicating their lives to good causes (Sullivan and Venter 2010). Therefore, they have often been conceptually connected to moral leadership. Goethals and Allison (2019) explored this link between heroism and moral leadership and stipulated that "all heroes are leaders, though not all leaders are heroes" (82). They make a distinction between non-heroic leaders, who are exclusionary—affirming a positive group identity at the expense of other segments of society—and heroic leaders, who are, without exception, inclusive, that is, looking beyond group boundaries to forge wider connections on the basis that we are all human beings.

The dominant image of moral leaders, often adopted by popular media, has emphasized personality-based notions that prescribe ethical behaviors with value-laden terms such as fair, trustworthy, respectful, pro-social, and transparent (e.g., Brown and Treviño 2006). Another popular notion of the moral leadership construct, especially in business contexts, stresses moral management—requiring compliance with a certain code (Neubert et al. 2009). However, neither of these frameworks captures the true complexities of moral leadership in today's world. A "trustworthy" or "respectful" leader can hold many different ideologies, permitting him/her to follow a wide range of, or even diametrically opposite, positions on ethical issues. Similarly, the compliance focus in the "moral management" approach does not consider that local norms and values in one context, such as an organization, may have actually drifted away from what is considered moral in a wider society. To address this complexity, Solinger and colleagues (2020) developed a process theory of moral leadership as a complex interplay between leaders, followers, and the societal context—encompassing the organization itself and larger societal frameworks such as family, religion, profession, the state, the market, and the community. A moral leader is then tasked with continually formulating and guarding an organization's "character" with respect to these wider frameworks and with mobilizing others in the organization to follow suit (see also Selznick 1957). According to this theory, moral leadership is not necessarily expressed by formal leaders or organizational managers. It can be the act by any party in assuming "an alternative, morally charged stance toward an issue" (Solinger et al. 2020, 15). Depending on situation and context, an individual can mobilize others and emerge as a moral leader. The more process-oriented perspective of Solinger and colleagues (2020) resonates with the conceptualization of hybrid heroes, as it regards heroes as changeable, even on the spectrum from scoundrel to saint.

The relationship between moral leaders and followers is pivotal for perceived heroism. According to Goethals and Allison (2019), moral leaders have undergone some form of personal transformation—reflecting Campbell's (1949) heroes' journey—yet, in order for them to be perceived as heroes, their followers should have experienced this transformation too, otherwise, a leader will be misunderstood and possibly be perceived as a villain. Conversely, followers who have been transformed will also perceive their untransformed leaders as villains (Goethals and Allison 2019). This model thus calls for congruence between leaders' and followers' attitudes, similar to relationship-oriented perspectives in management theory, such as leader-follower-exchange theory (Graen and Uhl-Bien 1995). No hero can exist without *other people* considering her/him as such. Heroes can emerge in moments of social change, and, similarly, heroes can fall when there is a paradigm shift. Thus, heroism is always bound by the perceptions of followers, which are tied to time and place.

Interestingly, many examples of modern hybrid heroes currently in leadership positions have a loyal and devoted following: the corrupt sales professional, who is glamorously celebrated in a Hollywood movie; the highly-praised business leader, who abuses personnel and relies on sweatshops for making profit; or the deceitful politician, who is admired for his brashness. Even people who are directly negatively affected by these hybrid heroes can be devoted fans.

This mechanism lays bare deep paradoxes of modern society, even absurdity at times (Bal et al. 2022), and a world where "obscene wealth is not looked down at, but perceived as an act of heroism" (8). Hybrid heroes, in the form of the rich, wealthy, and successful who get away with moral atrocities, are grounded on the fallacious logic of a just world, whereby wealth and success are earned by the individual, as are poverty, failure, and being in a marginalized position (Sandage 2009). Modern hybrid heroes—often powerful people with charisma, talent, and/or wealth—can thereby escape the system of justice as followers give them a "free pass" for crimes. In contrast, people on the outskirts of society—those who are *not* simultaneously perceived as heroes—are blamed for their tribulations and scrutinized with suspicion. When looking at hybrid heroes from a moral lens, it is important to raise awareness of the popularity of hybrid heroes and to see both sides of this archetype. Hybrid heroes are a phenomenon that should be analyzed, not normalized.

How Hybrid Hero Tales Could Stimulate Moral Leadership Development

> There is no coming to consciousness without pain. People will do anything, no matter how absurd, in order to avoid facing their own soul. One does not become enlightened by imagining figures of light, but by making the darkness conscious.
>
> *Carl Jung (1945, 335)*

There are numerous online articles claiming to present readers with the "7 best traits of a being a good leader" or "10 helpful habits that famous leaders have." These articles stress traits, habits, and characteristics, in line with traditional views of leadership, such as personality-based notions of prescribed ethical behaviors (e.g., Brown and Treviño 2006). When students in business schools begin leadership courses, they often internalized these one-dimensional conceptualizations. Yet, as emphasized in the previous sections, these perceptions miss the ambiguity of real life and the chaotic nature of leadership.

In recent years, diverse scandals in organizational life have fueled a public discussion on business ethics and the need for moral leadership. Part of this debate revolved around the development of moral leadership and the role that business schools have in educating their students for complex moral challenges (Ghoshal 2005; Giacalone and Thompson 2006). Critics claim that business schools pay too much attention to quantitative and mathematical skills, while overlooking soft skills such as self-reflection and personal development (Bennis and O'Toole 2005). Even when business schools teach ethics, they may sometimes (unintentionally) confirm an organization-centered instead of a human-centered worldview (Giacalone and Thompson 2006), whereby students learn to comply with dominant norms, such as profit-making, (Ghoshal 2005) and are not able to develop their own moral character.

My colleagues and I explored whether world literature could stimulate the moral development of business school students (Brokerhof et al. 2023). Narratives can mirror the "messiness" of real life, help people make sense of organizations (Patriotta 2003), and represent shared fantasies and collective emotions (Gabriel 2004). We envisioned that using world literature with protagonists facing complex moral challenges could stimulate students' awareness of moral complexity and their moral imagination—their subjective moral development (Brokerhof et al. 2023). For 13 weeks, MBA students in a business school in the Northeastern United States would privately read one work of world literature each week and discuss this in a group to "describe, analyze, judge and reflect" on the narrative (Sucher 2007). We inductively explored how students experienced the course, and through an in-depth grounded analysis, we discovered that they had developed "moral muscle," which we defined as "the dynamic individual capability for reflective moral action, characterized by moral sensitivity and sustained practice, in order to build and maintain moral character" (Brokerhof et al. 2023, 79). People showed different paths toward the development of moral muscle (i.e., some students started the course leaning toward moral absolutism and believing there was one right and one wrong, while others started the course leaning toward moral relativism, not believing that any objective right or wrong existed), yet all of them eventually developed a more complex grasp of what it means to be a moral leader. They moved away from pre-existing, one-dimensional images of leadership and understood that often moral decisions are not clean-cut in the moment they are made. They realized that growing moral muscle is an ongoing process. Similar to regular muscle, moral muscle needs to be trained in order to stay strong or grow. The literary narratives were a great means for training: they allowed students to reflect, invoked emotions, gave them an opportunity to learn from the perspectives of their peers, and helped expand their moral vocabulary (Brokerhof et al. 2023).

Interestingly, (fictional) characters who are most thought-provoking can often be regarded as hybrid heroes. In literary narratives, they are common. In the study mentioned above (Brokerhof et al. 2023), hybrid heroes sparked the most interesting discussions and helped students gain new insights. The story of Blessed Assurance by Allan Gurganus (1990), for instance, is an example of such a conflicted protagonist. The main character, Jerry, reflects on the period when he was 19 years old and had a job as a funeral insurance agent in a poor, black neighborhood. He worked in order to save money for his college tuition. The insurance company had doubtful moral standards: if clients could not pay two weeks in a row, they were kicked out of the insurance program no matter how long they had contributed in the past. Jerry tried to help his clients, but ultimately failed, leaving an older woman with whom he had developed a strong bond with to die without a funeral, despite years of payment. He left the job and went to college. In his career as a businessman (symbolically, in the laundry industry), he tries to do the ethically "right" thing, but he remains tormented by his past. As an older man, he visits a funeral of someone in a similar community today, someone he does not know, and pours his heart out in public. This story provoked intense discussions in the classroom and thereby opened students to new perspectives and interpretations of stories that differed from their own. It also catapulted them into the future as they asked themselves this question: How do I want to look back on my career and the moral decisions I make now?

The tales of hybrid heroes can help people confront their inner thoughts, moral struggles, and challenges—but *only* when they critically reflect on this hybridity. Above, I described research on the appeal of villain-hero Jordan Belfort of *The Wolf of Wall Street*, who was perceived, rather uncritically, as someone people would aspire to become (see Brokerhof 2021). This hybrid hero likely influenced the participants' career identity via the personal pathway, with little critical reflection (see Figure 1.1). Conversely, in the study with literary narratives in the business ethics classroom (Brokerhof et al. 2023), hybrid hero tales influenced students' career identity through deep reflection, group discussions, and emotional struggle. These stories likely influenced career identity through the reflective pathway (Figure 1.1). Critical and conscious reflection made students think about right and wrong and their own moral character—pondering who they were and who they wanted to become on a deeper level. Thus, it seems important that people not merely experience hybrid hero tales, but that they reflect on them and ideally discuss them in a diverse group. A cacophony of different perspectives could aid us in developing a notion close to Adam Smith's "impartial spectator" (Raphael 2007) and help broaden our repertoire of moral decision-making.

Where There Is Hope: How Hybrid Heroes can Sometimes Make Good Role Models

> We learn to become the narrator and the hero of our own story, without actually becoming the author of our own life.
>
> *Ricoeur (1991, 32)*

In this chapter, I have explained that hybrid hero tales can offer people opportunities to reflect on a deep level on fundamental and existential questions of identity—who they want to be in their own lives. The hybridity of heroes, their struggles, flaws, and dark side, show a more nuanced example of behavior. This image is less "flat" than superhero images of saint-like perfection, often out of reach for normal people. Without reflection or discussion, however, the lessons of hybrid hero tales might not be revealed, and uncritical absorption of villain-heroes, like Jordan Belfort, may even normalize corruption and encourage immoral behavior. It is therefore beneficial to be aware of the ubiquitous prevalence of hybrid hero tales in modern culture. Through awareness reflection and discussion, hybrid hero tales can offer an insight into how people act in the messiness of real life, how they can stray, but also get back on track. Group discussions of these complex characters can give new insights into different interpretations of the same character, whereby the same person might be considered a "hero" by some and a "villain" by others.

Another point highlighted in this chapter is the dynamic nature of hybrid heroes. Heroes rise and fall depending on how they are perceived in time, culture, and social context. This dynamism can inspire the debate on moral leadership. When we adopt the view of moral development as the growth of moral muscle, which needs to be trained by regular reflection and practice, it is helpful to *not* have a static image of a moral leader based on character traits but rather to regard people as moral or heroic when they can perform selfless *acts* that help others. Thus, we adopt a dynamic perspective on moral leadership (Solinger et al. 2020). Even though there may be downsides to moving away from traditional saint-like role models, we can still regard heroic leadership as a series of moral acts rather than a fixed state of being. The new concept of a hybrid hero spectrum can inspire people to explore new thresholds in behavior and to act morally in troublesome situations with the appropriate degree of reflection. Perhaps it is eye-opening to find both the hero and the villain in the same person and not fall into the trap of dichotomy and archetypes. As philosopher Alain Botton (2017) once said in a talk for the School of Life, "It is an immense psychological achievement when we can no longer merely divide people into absolutely 'brilliant, perfect, marvelous' and 'hateful, let me down, disappointed me' [...] We start off with idealization and we end up with denigration [...] Maturity is the ability to see that there are no heroes or sinners among human beings. All of us are this wonderfully perplexing mixture of the good and the bad."

References

Amper, Susan. 2010. Dexter's Dark World: The Serial Killer as Superhero. In *Serial Killers – Philosophy for Everyone: Being and Killing*, edited by Signe Waller, 103–113. West Sussex: Wiley–Blackwell.

Arsenault, Raymond. 1998. Wall Street (1987): The Stockbroker's Son and the Decade of Greed. *Film & History: An Interdisciplinary Journal of Film and Television Studies* 28, no. 1: 16–27.

Arthur, Michael B., Khapova, Svetlana N. and Richardson, Julia. 2016. *An Intelligent Career: Taking Ownership of Your Work and Your Life.* Oxford: Oxford University Press.

AZQuotes.com. 2024. Retrieved January 4, 2024, from AZQuotes: https://www.azquotes.com/author/81723-Tony_Meloto.

Bal, Matthijs, Brookes, Andy, Hack–Polay, Dieu, Kordowicz, Maria and Mendy, John. 2022. *The Absurd Workplace: How Absurdity is Normalized in Contemporary Society and the Workplace.* Cham: Springer Nature.

Bandura, Albert. 2002. Selective Moral Disengagement in the Exercise of Moral Agency. *Journal of Moral Education* 31, no. 2: 101–119.

Bauman, Zygmunt. 2013. *Liquid Modernity.* New York: John Wiley & Sons.

Belfort, Jordan. 2011. *The Wolf of Wall Street.* London: Hachette UK.

Bennis, Warren G. and O'Toole, Jim. 2005. How Business Schools Have Lost Their Way. *Harvard Business Review* 83, no. 5: 96–104.

Booker, Christopher. 2004. *The Seven Basic Plots: Why We Tell Stories.* London: A&C Black.

Botton, Alain de. 2017. Why You Will Marry the Wrong Person. *Google Zeitgeist*, 5 September. https://www.youtube.com/watch?v=DCS6t6NUAGQ.

Bröckling, Ulrich. 2019. Negations of the Heroic: A Typological Essay. *helden. heroes. héros.: E-Journal on Cultures of the Heroic*, special issue 5: 39–43.

Brokerhof, Inge M. 2020. Mentale Tijdreis Naar Je Future Work Self. *Tijdschrift voor Ontwikkeling in Organisaties* 10, no. 3: 70–76.

———. 2021. *Fictional Narratives at Work: How Stories Shape Career Identity, Future Work Selves and Moral Development.* Amsterdam Business Research Institute, Vrije Universiteit Amsterdam.

Brokerhof, Inge M., Bal, P. Matthijs, Jansen, Paul G. and Solinger, Omar N. 2018. Fictional Narratives and Identity Change: Three Pathways through which Stories influence the Dialogical Self. In *Dialogical Self: Inspirations, Considerations and Research*, edited by Malgorzata M. Puchalska-Wasyl, Piotr K. Oleś, and Hubert J. M. Hermans, 29–57. Lublin: Towarzystwo Naukowe KUL.

Brokerhof, Inge M., Sucher, Sandra J., Bal, P. Matthijs, Hakemulder, Frank, Jansen, Paul G. and Solinger, Omar N. 2023. Developing Moral Muscle in a Literature-Based Business Ethics Course. *Academy of Management Learning & Education* 22, no. 1: 63–87.

Brokerhof, Inge M., Ybema, Jan Fekke and Bal, P. Matthijs. 2020. Illness Narratives and Chronic Patients' Sustainable Employability: The Impact of Positive Work Stories. *PloS One* 15, no. 2: e0228581.

Brophy, Matthew. 2010. Sympathy for the Devil: Can a Serial Killer Ever Be Good? In *Serial Killers – Philosophy for Everyone: Being and Killing*, edited by Signe Waller, 78–89. West Sussex: Wiley–Blackwell.

Brown, Michael E. and Treviño, Linda K. 2006. Ethical Leadership: A Review and Future Directions. *The Leadership Quarterly* 17, no. 6: 595–616.

Brus, Anna, Knecht, Michi and Zillinger, Martin. 2020. Iconoclasm and the Restitution Debate. *HAU: Journal of Ethnographic Theory* 10, no. 3: 919–927.

Busselle, Rick and Bilandzic, Helena. 2009. Measuring Narrative Engagement. *Media Psychology* 12, no. 4: 321–347.

Campbell, Joseph. 1949. *The Hero with a Thousand Faces.* New York: Pantheon.

Carlson, Bronwyn and Farrelly, Terri. 2022. Monumental Changes: History Isn't Always Written by the Victors. *From the European South* 10: 11–24.

CBC. 2011. Twitchell Found Guilty of 1st-Degree Murder. 13 April. https://www.cbc .ca/news/canada/edmonton/twitchell-found-guilty-of-1st-degree-murder-1.998969.

Cinelli, Matteo, Quattrociocchi, Walter, Galeazzi, Alessandro, Valensise, Carlo M., Brugnoli, Emanuele, Schmidt, Ana L., Zola, Paola, Zollo, Fabiana and Scala, Antonio. 2020. The COVID-19 Social Media Infodemic. *Scientific Reports* 10, no. 1: 1–10.

Cinelli, Matteo, De Francisci Morales, Gianmarco, Galeazzi, Alessandro, Quattrociocchi, Walter and Starnini, Michele. 2021. The Echo Chamber Effect on Social Media. *Proceedings of the National Academy of Sciences* 118, no. 9: e2023301118.

Ferri, Anthony J. 2007. *Willing Suspension of Disbelief: Poetic Faith in Film*. Lanham: Lexington Books.

Fletcher, Joyce K. 2004. The Paradox of Postheroic Leadership: An Essay on Gender, Power, and Transformational. *The Leadership Quarterly* 15, no. 5: 647–661.

Fugate, Mel, Kinicki, Angelo J. and Ashforth, Blake E. 2004. Employability: A Psycho-Social Construct, Its Dimensions, and Applications. *Journal of Vocational Behavior* 65, no. 1: 1–38.

Gabriel, Yiannis. 2004. *Myths, Stories, and Organizations: Premodern Narratives for Our Times*. Oxford: Oxford University Press on Demand.

Gamboni, Dario. 2013. *The Destruction of Art: Iconoclasm and Vandalism since the French Revolution*. London: Reaktion Books.

Ghoshal, Sumantra. 2005. Bad Management Theories Are Destroying Good Management Practices. *Academy of Management Learning & Education* 4, no. 1: 75–91.

Giacalone, Robert A. and Thompson, Kenneth R. 2006. Business Ethics and Social Responsibility Education: Shifting the Worldview. *Academy of Management Learning & Education* 5, no. 3: 266–277.

Gibson, Donald E. 2004. Role Models in Career Development: New Directions for Theory and Research. *Journal of Vocational Behavior* 65, no. 1: 134–156.

Goethals, George R. and Allison, Scott T. 2019. *The Romance of Heroism and Heroic Leadership*. Bingley: Emerald Publishing Limited.

Graen, George B. and Uhl–Bien, Mary. 1995. Relationship-Based Approach to Leadership: Development of Leader-Member Exchange (LMX) Theory of Leadership over 25 Years: Applying a Multi-Level Multi-Domain Perspective. *The Leadership Quarterly* 6, no. 2: 219–247.

Guerrera, Francesco. 2010. How 'Wall Street' Changed Wall Street. *Financial Times*, 24 September. http://www.ft.com/intl/cms/s/2/7e55442a-c76a-11df-aeb1-00144 feab49a.html.

Gurganus, Allan. 1990. *White People*. New York: Ivy Books.

Hermans, Hubert J. 2014. Self as a Society of I-positions: A Dialogical Approach to Counseling. *The Journal of Humanistic Counseling* 53, no. 2: 134–159.

Ibarra, Herminia and Petriglieri, Jennifer L. 2010. Identity Work and Play. *Journal of Organizational Change Management* 23, no. 1: 10–25.

Investor Archive. 2020, November 11. *Warren Buffett | Bill Gates | Lecture | University of Washington* | 1998 [video]. Youtube. https://www.youtube.com/watch?v=R8VBTd2 R9nE.

Jung, Carl. 1945. *Alchemical Studies*. Princeton: Princeton University Press.

Kahneman, Daniel and Frederick, Shane. 2005. *A Model of Heuristic Judgment*. Cambridge: Cambridge University Press.

Kidd, David C. and Castano, Emanuele. 2013. Reading Literary Fiction Improves Theory of Mind. *Science* 342, no. 6156: 377–380.

Lindsay, Jeffry. 2004. *Darkly Dreaming Dexter (1)*. New York: Vintage Crime/Black Lizard.

Mandler, Jean M. 2014. *Stories, Scripts, and Scenes: Aspects of Schema Theory*. London: Psychology Press.

Markus, Hazel and Nurius, Paula. 1986. Possible Selves. *American Psychologist* 41, no. 9: 954.

Martin Del Campo, Michel. 2017. *Sympathy for the Devils: An Analysis of the Villain Archetype Since the Nineteenth Century*, Doctoral dissertation. Texas: Texas A&M International University.

McAdams, Dan P. 2008. Personal Narratives and the Life Story. In *Handbook of Personality: Theory and Research*, edited by Oliver P. John, Richard W. Robins and Lawrence A. Pervin, 242–262. New York: Guilford Press.

McDonald–Gibson, Charlotte. 2020. The Fight over "Black Pete" Brings a Reckoning on Racial Equality in the Netherlands. *Time Magazine*, 14 November. https://time.com /5910949/black-pete-netherlands-zwarte-piet/.

Meijers, Frans. 1998. The Development of a Career Identity. *International Journal for the Advancement of Counselling* 20, no. 3: 191–207.

Neubert, Mitchell J., Carlson, Dawn S., Kacmar, K. Michele, Roberts, James A. and Chonko, Lawrence B. 2009. The Virtuous Influence of Ethical Leadership Behavior: Evidence from the Field. *Journal of Business Ethics* 90: 157–170.

NOS. 2013. 2,1 miljoen mensen: Piet zo laten. 5 December. https://nos.nl/artikel /582940-2-1-miljoen-mensen-piet-zo-laten.

———. 2014. Rutte krijgt vraag over zwarte piet. 23 March. https://nos.nl/artikel /627085-rutte-krijgt-vraag-over-zwarte-piet.

Oatley, Keith. 1999. Meetings of Minds: Dialogue, Sympathy, and Identification, in Reading Fiction. *Poetics* 26, no. 5–6: 439–454.

Oshio, Atsushi. 2012. An All-or-Nothing Thinking Turns into Darkness: Relations Between Dichotomous Thinking and Personality Disorders. *Japanese Psychological Research* 54, no. 4: 424–429.

Parris, Denise L. and Welty Peachey, Jon. 2013. A Systematic Literature Review of Servant Leadership Theory in Organizational Context. *Journal of Business Ethics* 113, no. 3: 377–393.

Patriotta, Gerardo. 2003. Sensemaking on the Shop Floor: Narratives of Knowledge in Organizations. *Journal of Management Studies* 40, no. 2: 349–375.

Raphael, David D. 2007. *The Impartial Spectator: Adam Smith's Moral Philosophy*. Oxford: Clarendon Press.

Ricœur, Paul. 1991. Life in Quest of Narrative. In *On Paul Ricoeur: Narrative and Interpretation*, edited by David Wood, 20–33. London: Routledge.

Rowling, Joanne K. 2013. *Harry Potter and the Deathly Hallows*. London: Bloomsbury Publishing.

Ryömä, Arto. 2020. The Interplay of Heroic and Post-heroic Leadership: Exploring Tensions in Leadership Manifestations in the Oscillations between Onstage and Offstage Contexts. *Scandinavian Journal of Management* 36, no. 1: 1–15.

Salek, Thomas A. 2018. Money Doesn't Talk, It Swears: The Wolf of Wall Street as a Homology for America's Ambivalent Attitude on Financial Excess. *Communication Quarterly* 66, no. 1: 1–19.

Sandage, Scott A. 2009. *Born Losers*. Cambridge: Harvard University Press.

Selznick, Philip. 1957. *Leadership in Administration: A Sociological Interpretation*. New York: Harper & Row Publishers.

Slater, Michael D., Johnson, Benjamin K., Cohen, Jonathan, Comello, Maria Leonora G. and Ewoldsen, David R. 2014. Temporarily Expanding the Boundaries of the Self: Motivations for Entering the Story World and Implications for Narrative Effects. *Journal of Communication* 64, no. 3: 439–455.

Solinger, Omar N., Jansen, Paul G. and Cornelissen, Joep P. 2020. The Emergence of Moral Leadership. *Academy of Management Review* 45, no. 3: 504–527.

Sonenshein, Scott. 2007. The Role of Construction, Intuition, and Justification in Responding to Ethical Issues at Work: The Sensemaking-Intuition Model. *Academy of Management Review* 32, no. 4: 1022–1040.

Strauss, Karoline, Griffin, Mark A. and Parker, Sharon K. 2012. Future Work Selves: How Salient Hoped-for Identities Motivate Proactive Career Behaviors. *Journal of Applied Psychology* 97, no. 3: 580.

Sucher, Sandra. 2007. *Teaching the Moral Leader, a Literature-Based Leadership Course*. New York: Routledge.

Sullivan, Michael P. and Venter, Anre. 2010. Defining Heroes through Deductive and Inductive Investigations. *The Journal of Social Psychology* 150, no. 5: 471–484.

Van Tourhout, Benjamin. 2019. The Hybrid Hero: A Contagious Counterexample. *Journal of Humanistic Psychology* 59, no. 4: 540–567.

Wason, Peter C. 1968. Reasoning about a Rule. *Quarterly Journal of Experimental Psychology* 20, no. 3: 273–281.

Zelmerlöw, Måns. 2015. Heroes. *EBU European Broadcasting Union*, 23 May. https://www.youtube.com/watch?v=5sGOwFVUU0I.

Zillmann, Dolf. 1988. Mood Management through Communication Choices. *American Behavioral Scientist* 31: 327–340.

Chapter 2

ISN'T EVERY HEROIC PERSON ON A HYBRID JOURNEY? JOSEPH CAMPBELL REVISITED

By Stephan Sonnenburg

Joseph Campbell and the Hero's Journey

Joseph Campbell (1904–1987) was one of the most influential and creative mythographers. His most important achievement is no doubt the modeling of a single great story, which he calls the hero's journey. The basic motif is to leave one state of being and find a way to transform the social world into a richer condition. In his foundational work, *The Hero with a Thousand Faces*, Campbell (2008) regarded the monomyth as universal across time and cultural spaces. Therefore, he was less interested in cultural differences and contemporary fashions and trends but more in the discovery of the similarities and the common ground of myths as well as real or fictional stories. Although Campbell analyzed the elementary themes of myths and stories worldwide for common ground, he did point out that their expression is different in various sociocultural environments. Though myths resonate with local needs, they are revered by all people on earth, "appearing everywhere in new combinations, while remaining, like the elements of a kaleidoscope, only a few and always the same" (Campbell 2007, 15).

Campbell was deeply influenced by Jung's (1969) conceptualization of the archetype, Zimmer's (1992) mythological Indian studies, and in particular Rank's (1952) psychological approach to myths. His insights also parallel related developments in ritual theory offered by van Gennep (1960) and Turner (1969). Campbell's (1991) ideas were disseminated to a larger, non-academic audience by an interview series with Bill Moyers, which was broadcast one year after his death and published as *The Power of Myth*. Campbell's influence on popular culture is indisputable, and in fact, it was in the movies that he gained his greatest fame (Vogler 2007). His intellectual influence is readily apparent in the first Star Wars film trilogy (Campbell 1991, 2004). However, his multilayered work has not received enough acknowledgment from the academic community (Rensma 2009). As inspired by Campbell, heroism science emerged over the last decade as an interdisciplinary research field, and he is regarded as its founder (Allison and Goethals 2017).

Myths as Transparency to Transcendence

Myth "is the homeland of the inspiration" (Campbell 2007, 183) and belongs to the great treasures of humankind. It comprises the elementary thoughts, experiences, and ideas which have inspired and outlived societies and generations. Myths are the clues to the "spiritual potentialities of the human life" (Campbell 1991, 12). To open this treasure chest means to open human existence itself to the existential questions of life. Myths also offer a way to conduct oneself in harmony with one's nature. They are pathways to bliss (Campbell 2004), a deep sense of being and belonging on the path to self-discovery. If people follow their bliss, they have the possibility to live a mythologically inspired life (Campbell 2003). If someone is "in bliss," s/he is "on the edge of the transcendent already" (Campbell 2004, xxiii).

The concept of being beyond words and beyond images means that myths open people to transcendence beyond experience. In fact, Campbell (2003) ultimately defined a myth as a metaphor which is "transparent to transcendence" (51). Myths are expressions of the human imagination (Le Grice 2013), shaped by elementary archetypes imprinted in the psyche as the collective unconscious (Jung 1969). Moreover, archetypes are the motivating forces and references for the myths. They are universal to all of humankind.

However, what differentiates a myth from a story? The main difference is that stories are told, but myths are *experienced*. Myths always include the momentum of real presence, which means that they are enacted, often in rites or rituals. "A ritual is nothing but the dramatic, visual, active manifestation or representation of a myth. By participating in the rite, you are engaged in the myth, and the myth works on you—provided, of course, that you are caught by the image." (Campbell 2004, 97) If enacted this way, myths fulfill their function and help human beings to experience themselves, the social order, as well as the universe, in a mystical way.

Even if myths vary in place and time, Campbell (2008) explained in *The Hero with a Thousand Faces* that there is one principal myth in the world, which he marked as the monomyth. He believed that all myths emerge out of a common creative imagination: the human search for ultimate spiritual meaning, paralleling the legends of heroes who journey to an unknown world and battle with the powers of darkness in order to return with the gift of knowledge for society. The ultimate spiritual meaning is shared by all. Thus, we can say that the hero with a thousand faces could be also seen as a thousand heroes with one spirit.

The Hero's Journey as a Generic Narrative Framework

Campbell's observations lead to the development of the hero's journey, at once the illustration and holistic framework for the monomyth. The hero's journey describes the stages of a transformation as a narrative pattern that can appear physically, psychologically, emotionally and spiritually. The narrative prototype is both simplistic and rich in possible interpretations. This can be seen in the different applications of the theory across the humanities, psychology, and cultural studies. As Campbell (2004) said, the motifs of the hero's journey appear not only in myth and literature, but also in the plot of everyone's life.

Over the past 30 years, Campbell's work on the hero's journey has made its way into various academic and professional areas and domains. Vogler (2007), for instance, Campbell's main disciple, used it for narrative analysis and composition of films and plays. Rebillot (1993) developed it further into a gestalt therapeutic concept and a broader psychological approach for personal renewal, focusing on the hero as a universal transformative archetype as described by Pearson (1991). The hero's journey has also been employed as a metaphor in learning and education (Brown and Moffett 1999; Goldstein 2005), in organizational change and leadership (Allison and Goethals 2017), as well as in law (Robbins 2006). It even serves as a conceptual springboard for the development of computer games (Buchanan–Oliver and Seo 2012) and it finds its way into esotericism (Banzhaf 2000).

As Allison and Goethals (2017) explain, the description of the hero's journey "points to three distinct transformations: A transformation of setting, a transformation of self, and a transformation of society [...] Without a change in setting, the hero cannot change herself, and without a change in herself, the hero cannot change the world" (381). In its original pattern, the hero's journey contains 17 stages, encompassing three main phases: departure, initiation, and return. When we first meet the hero, he resides in the ordinary world until he receives the call to adventure. The individual is at first reluctant (refusal of the call). Next, a mentor (supernatural aid) encourages him to depart. Then, the crossing of the first threshold enables the hero to enter the special and unknown world (the belly of the whale) for initiation. Here, the individual encounters tests, allies, and enemies (the road of trials) and approaches the inmost cave (the meeting with the goddess, a woman as the temptress) to endure the ordeal (atonement with the father, apotheosis).

Thereafter, the hero receives a reward as the ultimate boon. He may be tempted to rest at this stage, believing that he has already gained all things ever desired (refusal of the return). However, it is vital to return. After further challenges in the special world (the magic flight, rescue from without), the hero crosses the return threshold to re-enter the ordinary world. The hero experiences a resurrection and becomes a master of the two worlds (e.g., spiritual and ordinary). Finally, the ultimate boon benefits the ordinary world— thereafter enhancing freedom (Campbell 2008). Yet, Allison and Goethals (2017) claim that all hero's journeys do not contain the same dynamics. They can vary with regard to subject (hero or follower(s)), entity (individual, dyad, group, organization, or society), speed (slow or fast), duration (short-lived or long-lasting), life phase (early, middle, or late), type (moral, emotional, spiritual, intellectual, physical, and/or motivational), depth (shallow or deep), or source (internal or external).

In the Appendix (Campbell 2008), there is an illustration of the hero's journey. However, one can see that this is only loosely connected to the afore description, though it will be interesting for those who want to explore this further. Moreover, this illustration shows that even though Campbell frequently varied his descriptions of the hero's journey, the core elements remain constant (Vogler 2007). Essential variations of Campbell's stages are the nine-step model of creative self-experience (Rebillot 1993) or the twelve-stage skeletal framework for writers (Vogler 2007). Banzhaf (2000) added a new context in combining it with the 22 tarot cards of the major arcana. Campbell already foresaw the benefits of this combination with tarot:

> The most interesting question I ever got was when I was lecturing here at Esalen [...] in 1967. Somebody asked, 'What about the symbolism of the Waite deck of tarot cards?' Well, I hadn't thought about it. [...] That was a very exciting thing, I had the luck to recognize a couple of sequences there. There is one for the Four Ages of Man: Youth, Maturity, Age, and what Dante calls Senility. [...] And then the big set at the end, the Honors Suit, the Major Arcana, has to do with the mystical path. It worked out just like that; it was right in front of my face. It was a fascinating experience, the most interesting I have had here. [...] I saw it there, what it represented was a program for life that derived from European medieval consciousness. And actually carried into symbolic form many of the implications of Dante's philosophy. That was the one that really hit me. Campbell (2003, 172–175)

Since the stages are closely anchored in the human psyche (Banzhaf 2000), the hero's journey has the potential to help people address many kinds of challenges. Banzhaf (2000) even considered it as a personal guide for an individual's life path. The framework can help people reflect on their own lives. When confronted with seemingly unsolvable problems, they often have the feeling they are the only ones who have ever faced issues of the sort. However, they will discover that many others have already experienced similar situations. As a blueprint, the hero's journey demonstrates that overcoming challenges is an important part of life and that transformation often follows the process. Almost all of us experience multiple hero journeys with varying degrees of metamorphosis.

A Transformative Reflection of the Hero's Journey

The hero's journey is a strong metaphor for building confidence and courage and for encouraging change and transformation. The combination of coincidence, universality, simplicity, and the variety and richness in one narrative pattern are very powerful. However, there are flaws in the frameworks, which lead to the questions discussed in the following section.

Is it always the journey of a hero?

Any person who completes the journey is transformed and, therefore, can be regarded as an improved version of his previous self. This new identity can be fictional or real, can involve a superhero or ordinary hero, who is engaged or even hidden. In Campbell's oeuvre, there is a strong focus on men as heroes, overlooking the role of heroines. However, it should be noted that when his book *The Hero with a Thousand Faces* was first published in 1949, it was a time when women were far from equal in society. That is why we should now talk about female and male heroes, or even use the terms "heroes" and "heroines."

Campbell addresses primarily individuals, yet the question arises if the hero's journey can be applied to group settings, which is more in line with postheroic leadership focusing on teams and collectives (Ryömä 2020). A traveler is often supported by companions, and they can be so prominent that it does not make sense to differentiate between them and the hero. An illustrative fictional example is *The Lord of the Rings* (Tolkien 2004), in which there is not one single hero but a constellation of them who go together on an adventurous journey.

Inspired by all human possibilities, I suggest "heroic journey" as an alternative to "hero's journey." This avoids the bias toward the male hero and allows us to regard every person equally, either singly or in a group, as they undertake the journey. In addition, the adjective "heroic" avoids a subject orientation and highlights the performative and situational components of the journey, as it is more about the transformative process for the people.

Is there a clear sequence of stages during the hero's journey?

Although the number of stages varies in Campbell's oeuvre, the sequence is the key characteristic of the hero's journey in a basic pattern of departure, initiation, and return. Over recent decades, this sequential model has been simplified, streamlined, and adapted to fit the needs of specific professional domains and scientific disciplines. Yet all relevant models of the hero's journey (Rebillot 1993; Campbell 2004; Vogler 2007) focus on a sequential order, in particular with regard to departure and initiation. In addition, a deeper description of the return stages is missing in the models.

Following Allison and Goethals (2017), the hero's journey involves setbacks, fears, suffering, and a kind of dying of the former self. Although the transformation of the hero is the most important aspect, the exact nature of the process and the way the ultimate boon is integrated into the ordinary world at the journey's end are often overlooked. Especially when applying the strict sequence of stages to real life, beyond the fictional world, it is not clear what should really happen at each stage and whether the stages are necessary in the first place. The main conceptual difference between the heroic journey described in the next section lies in a better balance between departure, initiation, and return, as well as hybridity between the stages.

Is the goal of the hero's journey always sainthood?

Heroes in the traditional meaning are "almost always highly moral, and they are generally very competent and effective" (Goethals and Allison 2019, 2). Although they face obstacles and challenges, they should never look back and always move forward in a kind of Darwinian mode of transformation. During their journeys, the heroes are regarded as saints, diametrically opposed to the villains who hinder or even endanger them. This dichotomy is still the dominant view in literature. Unlike heroes who want to unify the world, villains want to divide humans (Goethals and Allison 2019).

The question arises if this dichotomy still really applies. Although consistently used in culture to establish moral standards, a hero is only a social construct subject to change: "[H]eroes of one era may prove to be villains in another time when controverting evidence emerges [...] Moreover, the very same act accorded hero status in one group, such as suicide bombing, is absolutely abhorrent to many others" (Franco et al. 2011, 99).

Vogler (2007) explicitly describes the tension a hero faces on her or his journey as s/he changes and grows. This often involves a vacillation between despair and hope, weakness and strength, folly and wisdom, love and hate, or, in other words, between the natures of a scoundrel and a saint. Therefore, the heroic journey should be regarded as hybrid, as the character transforms and swings back and forth between the two poles.

The Hybrid Heroic Journey

Inspired by the transformative reflection of the journey, I have developed a new framework, which I call the *hybrid heroic journey*. This concept combines insights from the following sources: 12 revised stages of the classical hero's journey (Rebillot 1993; Campbell 2004; Vogler 2007), 12 selected archetypes (Hartwell and Chen 2012), and 21 cards (the zero card has a special role) of the major arcana of tarot (Banzhaf 2000).

Figure 2.1 introduces the basic outline of the hybrid heroic journey. It no longer consists of a circle of stages in perfect harmony or symmetry but rather assumes an elliptical shape to illustrate that a journey is chaotic, unpredictable, and never fully structured. In contrast to a simple stage model, the hybrid

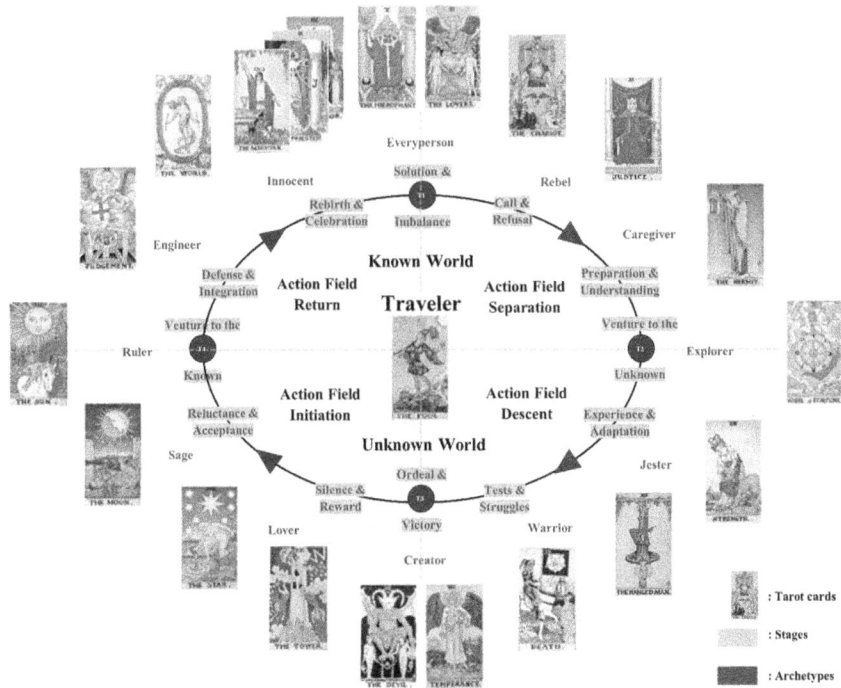

Figure 2.1 Framework of the hybrid heroic journey.

heroic journey involves four action fields which can be assigned to the known or unknown world: separation, descent, initiation, and return. These fields are framed by four turning points (T1 to T4) and consist of stages supported by archetypes and cards from the major arcana of tarot.

Although the action fields still consist of stages (e.g., call & refusal), they should not be considered as sequential but rather interconnected through dynamics (the archetypes and tarot), reflecting both the course and the hybrid character of the journey, characterized by polarized forces that influence the travelers. This "attracts our attention initially because we all perceive that our lives are sawed back and forth by similar contradictions and conflicts, tugging us in many directions at once along multiple lines of polarity, such as man and wife, parent and children, employee and boss, individual and society" (Vogler 2007, 318).

Polarity is a fundamental principle that generates tension and emotional responses for the traveler, leading to growth, albeit often in a painful manner. We can differentiate between four types of tension: internal, as seen through ambivalent feelings and thoughts; inter-personal, involving conflict between two actors; external, between actor and society; and cosmic, as a collision between an actor and a supernatural entity (Singh and Sonnenburg 2012). In practice, it is often difficult to distinguish the four categories as they coexist and commingle.

Archetypes and tarot

Although Campbell regarded archetypes and the tarot as motivating forces for the myths, he did not explore their relevance and potential for developing the hero's journey further. Both are essential components of the hybrid heroic journey that push us into metaphorical thinking, which supports human understanding. This assumption is supported by research suggesting that metaphors may form the basis for thoughts, perceptions, and social experiences (Lakoff and Johnson 2003).

Archetypes describe the travelers' mood and mindset, which guide and inspire them along the journey. The choice of the 12 archetypes has a speculative momentum but is based on the conflation of three basic typologies (Jung 1969; Pearson 1991; Hartwell and Chen 2012). Representing personalities as opposed to abstract principles, archetypes are laden with meaning and impel us to dig deeper into the dynamics of feelings, in particular via their representation in stories and myths. "We recognize the archetypes. They are familiar, part of the human family. They speak to us" (Hartwell and Chen 2012, 1). Moreover, they simultaneously reassure and challenge us, as we struggle to manage the conflicting messages.

The major arcana of the tarot also represents archetypes which are motifs symbolizing a person's path in life. The 21 cards of the major arcana form a clear sequence. It has a deep meaning, is the central heart of the tarot, in an archetypal pattern of a range of actions woven from the 21 motifs, as a clear guide for personal orientation. These motifs are insights "that are secret in their nature because they have been gained from the essential, yet invisible, correlations behind the outer world of appearances, from the reality behind the reality [...] At its center is the question about an individual's path in life and the meaning of death" (Banzhaf 2000, 7). The major arcana regards reality as a duality of opposing forces (e.g., life and death, female and male, creation and destruction, light and darkness, parents and children, or individuals and society), with each pole a reference point for the other. Heroes must address this polarity to discover the meaning as s/he attempts to balance the disparate forces.

The heroic person as a fool

Isn't it strange that a heroic person can also be seen as a fool? Generally speaking, heroes are considered in a different way: courageous, strong, clever, and always surrounded by the aura of the eternal saint, even if they are not smart or skillful at the outset of their journeys. In particular, in fairy tales, the fools are often the youngest or most inexperienced characters, possibly even outlaws. However, they grow up very fast as long as they follow the path to sainthood.

When we observe the traveler as a fool, we begin to understand the hybrid texture of the heroic journey. The fool is both deprecated and valued, despised and tolerated, ridiculed and enjoyed, degraded, and privileged. Yet s/he has no biases or mental blocks because s/he is always open to new insights and experiences. As an archetype, s/he represents the playful child within us and displays a willingness to make mistakes on the pathway to learning and transformation. The dog on the fool's tarot card symbolizes the importance of feelings, instincts, and senses during the journey but also the need to remain alert to avoid catastrophes or madness. Thus, the heroic fool needs to find a balance between playfulness and reflection.

Turning point of the known

At the beginning of the journey, a problem or, better said, a challenge emerges in the known world, in an imbalanced situation that is usually seen and mostly felt, even if unconsciously, by the traveler. It might be a crisis or an opportunity which needs to be exploited for its educational value. Therefore, the imbalance can be triggered by a negative or positive impulse. Imbalance can best be described as a recurring void in everyday life that causes angst. Even if the challenge is related to other people and not at all to the traveler, it has to be internalized. The problem is like a signal that there is a reason to start the journey.

At this turning point, most people are in a mood or mindset symbolized by the archetype "everyperson," as well as the tarot cards "hierophant" and "lovers." Their combined dynamic could be characterized as follows: The everyperson feels a strong sense of belonging to the known world. S/he wants to do the right thing without heroics or adventures and prefers to be under-stated, nonthreatening, helpful, and loyal to the community. Though preoc-cupied by the basic routines of life, s/he looks up to others who are perhaps more experienced, and s/he begins to move away from the initial feeling of unity and connectedness with the known world. S/he realizes that s/he is different and begins to search for a new meaning. However, the danger is that the everyperson can easily be influenced by others whom s/he regards as "gurus." To become a true traveler and heroic person, the everyperson needs to assert her/his own free will and express deeply felt emotions.

Action field of separation

Still in the known world, awareness of imbalance increases to such a great extent that the traveler experiences a clear call for action. It is now fully evi-dent to her/him that it is necessary to change the current situation. However, despite the strong urge for change, there is often an instinctive reaction to refuse this impulse and to continue with the day-to-day routines in the security of the familiar world. S/he might feel uncertain about the tasks and unknown difficulties that could possibly be experienced during the journey, or s/he may be inhibited by the need to remain within the confines of an overused efficiency–effectiveness dichotomy that impedes creativity for the sake of sav-ing time. In addition, conflicts are likely to occur between the traveler and others who have different perceptions and expectations. Yet with the help of a mentor, who gives her/him support and strength and who emphasizes the importance of the journey, the traveler finally accepts the call and leaves the comfort zone to overcome the fear of the unknown.

The traveler should be aware that s/he cannot enter the unknown world without a full understanding of the challenge. Information about the current situation must be collected from various sources. Furthermore, the traveler needs to acquire and learn certain skills, which can be useful during the jour-ney. S/he needs to feel stronger, well-equipped, and confident for the next turning point and action field. It should be clear that preparation for the upcoming challenges and circumstances takes time. It would be naive to rush through and take everything for granted. During the stage of "preparation & understanding," the traveler usually starts to perceive the seriousness of the decision.

In the action field of separation, the traveler is in the mood or mindset of the archetypes "rebel" and "caregiver," as well as the tarot cards of "chariot," "justice," and "hermit." Their combined dynamic could be characterized as follows: The traveler starts to question the status quo of the known world and develops a mindset of critical thinking. S/he stands up for her/himself without denying the old character and personality. The traveler should find others in the known world who can support her/him to bring issues to the forefront and cope with all the concerns related to the journey. S/he is fully aware that the familiar is characterized by dualities, with opposing poles that constantly create tension which needs to be balanced. From a hybrid perspective, it is important not to select a side and judge one extreme as good and right and the other as bad and wrong. S/he needs to embrace and master the contradictions and be responsible for the upcoming course of the journey.

Turning point of venture to the unknown world

The challenge for a heroic person is to define a point of view, perhaps a creative insight or a precise problem statement, helping her/him move forward as s/he travels from the known world to the unknown world. Forging this creative insight for the journey is betwixt the known and the unknown, therefore complicated. On the one hand, it should reflect the current situation and what the traveler already knows, while on the other, it should allow what is not known yet to appear on the horizon. The venture to the unknown is fraught with tension, again a situation of polarized forces. The traveler wants to actively start the journey but the entrance to the unknown world is blocked by a threshold, which, once crossed, symbolizes the active "start" of the hybrid heroic excursion, a point of no return. This is "the moment the wheels leave the ground and the plane begins to fly" (Vogler 2007, 131).

The would-be hero/heroine has to be prepared for any contingency as s/he ventures forth to places where other less hardy souls fear to tread. Among other obstacles, s/he will face guardians standing at either side of the entrances to holy places in the form of lions, bulls or fearsome warriors with uplifted weapons. They are there to keep out the so-called "spoilsports," the advocates of Aristotelian logic, for whom A can never be B (Campbell 2007). At the same time, the traveler needs to overcome her/his fears and self-doubt and must accept the loss of security and routine in order to gain something new. S/he needs to leave the past behind and focus on the future as s/he takes responsibility for the decision to move ahead.

At the turning point of "venture to the unknown," the traveler is in a mood or mindset symbolized by the archetype "explorer" as well as the tarot card "wheel of fortune." Their combined dynamic could be characterized as follows: a powerful craving for new experiences, even not knowing what is coming next. There is no limit to becoming and no end to learning. The traveler leaves the comfort of the known world and hits the open road where s/he needs to align new outer realities with inner needs. Only after s/he has become aware of her/his true identity, is s/he mature enough to ask "what is the task" and to search for answers. Along the way s/he must be open to thinking, sensing, feeling, and intuition to promote understanding.

Action field of descent

The journey through the unknown world, after the separation from the known, is the major adventurous challenge. The traveler must develop familiarity with the new world as a prelude to full engagement. That means adapting to the different rules, rhythms, values, and priorities of the new environment (Vogler 2007). Moreover, the traveler needs to be aware that the unknown world presents unforeseen and unimaginable dynamics, so s/he should rely on their skills and intuition. Through first experiences, which could be regarded as trial and error, the traveler gains more personal awareness and consciousness about her/himself, the situation, its rules, and its circumstances. During "experience & adaptation," it is clear that one cannot prepare for every possible event and that one should trust one's intuition and feelings.

After this period of adjustment, the traveler is confronted with the first tests, often accompanied by tensions and disagreements. The tensions, as described above, might be internal, inter-personal, external, or cosmic. This is a particularly challenging time for the traveler, as she/he needs to develop enough self-confidence to continue. Often, through the help of allies and friends, s/he musters more courage and confidence for the upcoming turning points and action fields. The biggest challenge is to confront obstacles without trying to escape. Setbacks must be anticipated so that s/he does not leave the unknown world too early. During the stage of "tests & struggles," the idea-generating potential should be strengthened, and each traveler should be enabled to unfold her/his creativity.

In the action field of descent, the traveler is in a mood or mindset characterized by the archetypes "jester" and "warrior," as well as the tarot cards "strength," "hanged man," and "death." Their combined dynamic could be characterized as follows: The traveler develops and strengthens ego powers so that s/he can deal with the unknown world. S/he also needs to overcome the critical inner voice. Motivated to experiment or play, the traveler turns things on their head, appreciates change, surprise, and even wicked intelligence. The fool residing inside is now fully developed as it comes to the surface, and this leads to an open attitude toward the unconscious. There is nothing more to be learned, only immersion in the creative flow of the heroic journey. However, the journey is still uncertain and uncomfortable at this stage. During the descent, the traveler experiences fears of destruction, loneliness, or the meaninglessness of life. However, this is only the beginning of letting things go and creating something new. The traveler becomes involved with her/his opposite poles and overcomes the ego to forge a higher self.

Turning point of the unknown

Now, the traveler is ready to approach her/his greatest challenge, the ordeal of the hybrid heroic journey. This stage, the third turning point, either brings great fear, the ultimate enemy, or a fundamental crisis. All travelers must believe in themselves and be strong enough to persevere. They often experience failures before achieving victory because "sometimes things have to get worse before they can get better" (Vogler 2007, 157). However, it takes more than courage and confidence to prevail at this stage. The traveler can be successful only if s/he comes up with fresh and creative ways to face the ordeal. By overcoming the challenges, often with confidence gained from the previous struggles, s/he transforms more and more into a "real" heroic fool. The stage of "ordeal & victory" is the journey's peak and represents the aha—moment when one senses that one has found a great idea or solution, or something of high value in the environment of the unknown world.

At the turning point of the unknown, the traveler is in a mood or mindset symbolized by the archetype "creator" as well as the tarot cards "temperance" and "devil." Their combined dynamic is as follows: The traveler deals with the negative sides of her/his personality. S/he frees her/himself from addictions. Finally, the traveler brings polarized forces together into equilibrium. S/he overcomes this by believing in the value of inner expression as well as the power to create meaning. The risk, however, is that the traveler may be trapped in the middle of the unknown world in a struggle for perfection.

Action field of initiation

The climax of the ordeal can be elusive. Even though an impressive victory might be achieved, it should be clear for the traveler that s/he is only halfway through her/his journey. Therefore, it is time to take a break, regain energy, and reflect upon the current situation, the achievements to date, and the implications for the future. It is also a moment of pride in the accomplishments. Thoughtful silence may help the traveler understand and appreciate the reward. The stage of "silence & reward" calls for one step back to understand what has happened from a distant perspective and to see the bigger picture of the reward ahead.

It is now time for the traveler to bring the reward back to the known world. However, s/he might be enamored by the charm of the new world so much that s/he might not want to return to the familiar realm, which might seem boring and dull by comparison. There is now a danger that s/he could become pompous and overconfident. In the end, sometimes with external encouragement, the traveler realizes that s/he needs to return, partly because the reward would be useless if it was not carried back for the benefit of the known world. During the stage of "reluctance & acceptance," the traveler must accept the path lying before her/him and should be ready for the second half of the journey.

In the action field of initiation, s/he is in a mood or mindset symbolized by the archetypes "lover" and "sage" as well as the tarot cards "tower," "star," and "moon." Their combined dynamic could be characterized as follows: The traveler seizes the reward, which is a breakthrough to greater freedom. Enjoying the moment of victory, s/he feels renewed and refreshed with a deeper sense of identity. However, s/he needs to critically analyze the current situation and understand that s/he cannot stand still for long. To move on, the traveler needs to balance change with stability. She/he needs to understand the bigger picture, the unity behind the polarized forces.

Turning point of venture to the known world

The traveler leaves the unknown world and returns to the known world, where s/he faces the old familiar circumstances. This fourth turning point, like the venture to the unknown, involves a tricky threshold. The challenge is to find a way back in order to explain and integrate the reward in the known world. This stage demonstrates that the reward is only valuable if it is applied in the known world in a way that facilitates a transformation.

At the turning point of "venture to the known," the traveler is in a mood or mindset symbolized by the archetype "ruler" as well as the tarot card "sun." Their combined dynamic could be characterized as follows: To cross the threshold from unknown to known, the traveler needs to develop a mindset mixing the forces of power, responsibility, benevolence, and reconciliation. This establishes a framework for the reward to transform the known world.

Action field of return

Now, the traveler returns to the known world with the reward. S/he needs to realize that s/he cannot rest on laurels. The last challenge comes from critics who might try to undermine the achievements or refuse the reward in the context of the not-invented-here syndrome. It is incumbent on the traveler to present the reward in such a way that others understand it and can easily integrate it into a rational life. This is very difficult. In fact, this can be even more grueling than descending into your own depths in the first place (Campbell 2004). Therefore, the traveler has to defend the reward and its beneficial virtue. The stage of "defense & integration" reminds her/him of all the tests and ordeals in the unknown world and reveals whether s/he has truly understood the lesson of the hybrid heroic journey. The reward can only unfold its transformative power if others are aware of its benefits and if it is incorporated into the fabric of the known world.

This process leads to a transformation akin to the rebirth of the traveler her/himself in the known world. It involves a new sense of balance and comfort as s/he recalls the positive elements of the hybrid heroic journey. Now it is time to celebrate the achievements and appreciate the rebirth. For the traveler, this is an emotional prerequisite so that s/he is willing to start a new journey in the future, which I call the Odysseus quest effect.

In the action field of return, the traveler is in a mood or mindset symbolized by the archetypes "engineer" and "innocent," as well as the tarot cards "judgement," "the world," and the heavenly ("magician" and "high priestess") and earthly ("empress" and "emperor") parents. Their combined dynamic could be characterized as follows: The traveler becomes results-driven, focuses on making things work, and orients her/himself so that the reward is finally at the right place. This can be regarded as a kind of healing of the known world. The reward becomes tangible, takes form, and resonates with the rhythm of the four parents. Together, they finally reflect upon the hybrid heroic journey as a precursor leading to the transformation in the known world.

The hybrid heroic journey has served its purpose when the reward heals the imbalance in the known world. The traveler has fulfilled her/his mission. The regained balance and harmony not only enable her/him to enjoy the moment but also to focus on new challenges. As visualized in Figure 2.2, the solution is regarded as a part of the first stage of the journey. Yet the process continues unfolding as the solution causes a new imbalance in a way that initiates the next journey. In other words, each end morphs into a beginning, leading to a cyclic view of the hybrid heroic journey. The archetype of the everyperson reinforces this understanding, as the traveler starts and ends as an everyperson. But through the knowledge and experience gained during the journey, the traveler has strengthened the attributes of her/his personality and has become a heroic everyman. You never start from the same zero. It is always a new zero to become a heroic fool.

Numbers and the elliptic shape of the hybrid heroic journey

The question arises: Why are there 12 stages and archetype cards, or actually 13, and what is the importance of the number 21, which resonates with the major arcana (the fool as the traveler is the 22nd card). One counts the last stage of solution upon the return, conjoined with the first stage of imbalance, when the journey continues with the integration of the solution. There is no logical reason but only a mythological explanation for the 13 stages and the relevance of 21, which together symbolize continuous change and transformation. Campbell explained (see Figure 2.2) the significance of the numbers:

> Now back to the Great Seal. When you count the number of ranges on this pyramid, you find there are thirteen. And when you come to the bottom, there is an inscription in Roman numerals. It is, of course, 1776. Then, when you add one and seven and seven and six, you get twenty-one, which is the age of reason, is it not? It was in 1776 that the thirteen states declared independence. The number thirteen is the number of transformation and rebirth. At the Last Supper there were twelve apostles and one Christ, who was going to die and be reborn. Thirteen is the number of getting out of the field of the bounds of twelve into the transcendent. You have the twelve signs of the zodiac and the sun. These men were very conscious of the number thirteen as the number

Figure 2.2 Reverse of the Great Seal. Kevkhiev Yury, Dreamstime.

of resurrection and rebirth and new life, and they played it up here all the way through. (Campbell and Moyers 1991, 32)

Speaking of the heroic fool once again, it is an appropriate time to return to a discussion of the ellipse (see Figure 2.1 again) and its deviation from the perfect circular form, which is the standard model of the hero's journey. In particular, perfection may often be a desired goal but is probably more of a dream which, is itself hybrid: neither good nor bad. What is significant, however, is that the fool and even the heroic fool are unlikely to achieve perfection. Moreover, imbalance is the alpha and omega of the journey and is an integral and necessary stage for transformation. The goal is not perfection, but the absence of perfection, and we need to keep this in mind to avoid bogging down in an attempt to attain the unattainable. Therefore, the ellipse is the chosen form for the heroic journey to represent progress, in contrast to the perfection of the traditional circle model.

The narrator's paradox is that s/he must tell the heroic journey in linear, chronological, and typically idealistic terms, all the time knowing that the process is cyclical and more complex than it appears. In fact, a heroic fool needs several cyclical actions for transformation, but not much has been written about the need to undergo the process more than once. The ellipse shows that the journey itself is the main focus and that the end is simply one of several other stages. Therefore, the greatness of the heroic fool emerges during the process and not at the finale. In other words, it is not about being a hero but about becoming heroic. "We don't ever 'get there'. We are always 'getting there'" (Brown and Moffett 1999, 2).

References

Allison, Scott T. and Goethals, George R. 2017. The Hero's Transformation. In *Handbook of Heroism and Heroic Leadership*, edited by Scott T. Allison, George R. Goethals and Roderick M. Kramer, 379–400. New York: Routledge.

Banzhaf, Hajo. 2000. *Tarot and the Journey of the Hero*. York Beach: Samuel Weiser.

Brown, John L. and Moffett, Cerylle A. 1999. *The Hero's Journey: How Educators Can Transform Schools and Improve Learning*. Alexandria: ASCD.

Buchanan–Oliver, Margo and Seo, Yuri. 2012. Play as Co-Created Narrative in Computer Game Consumption: The Hero's Journey in Warcraft III. *Journal of Consumer Behaviour* 11, no. 6: 423–431.

Campbell, Joseph. 1991. *The Masks of God: Primitive Mythology*. New York, NY: Penguin Compass.

———. 2003. *The Hero's Journey: Joseph Campbell on his Life and Work*. Novato: New World Library.

———. 2004. *Pathways to Bliss: Mythology and Personal Transformation*. Novato: New World Library.

————. 2007. *The Mythic Dimension: Selected Essays 1959–1987*. Novato: New World Library.

————. 2008. *The Hero with a Thousand Faces (3rd Edition)*. Novato: New World Library.

Campbell, Joseph and Moyers, Bill. 1991. *The Power of Myth*. New York: Anchor Books.

Franco, Zeno E., Blau, Kathy and Zimbardo, Philip G. 2011. Heroism: A Conceptual Analysis and Differentiation between Heroic Action and Altruism. *Review of General Psychology* 15, no. 2: 99–113.

Goethals, George R. and Allison, Scott T. 2019. *The Romance of Heroism and Heroic Leadership*. Bingley: Emerald Publishing.

Goldstein, Lisa S. 2005. Becoming a Teacher as a Hero's Journey: Using Metaphor in Preservice Teacher Education. *Teacher Education Quarterly* 32, no. 1: 7–24.

Hartwell, Margaret P. and Chen, Joshua C. 2012. *Archetypes in Branding: A Toolkit for Creatives and Strategists*. Ohio: HOW Books.

Jung, Carl G. 1969. *The Archetypes and the Collective Unconscious*. London: Routledge.

Lakoff, George and Johnson, Mark. 2003. *Metaphors We Live By*. London: University of Chicago Press.

Le Grice, Keiron. 2013. *The Rebirth of the Hero: Mythology as a Guide to Spiritual Transformation*. London: Muswell Hill Press.

Pearson, Carol S. 1991. *Awakening the Heroes Within: Twelve Archetypes to Help Us Find Ourselves and Transform the World*. New York: HarperOne.

Rank, Otto. 1952. *The Myth of the Birth of the Hero: A Psychological Interpretation of Mythology*. New York: R. Brunner.

Rebillot, Paul. 1993. *The Call to Adventure: Bringing the Hero's Journey to Daily Life*. San Francisco: Harper Collins.

Rensma, Ritske. 2009. *The Innateness of Myth: A New Interpretation of Joseph Campbell's Reception of C. G. Jung*. New York: Continuum.

Robbins, Ruth A. 2006. Harry Potter, Ruby Slippers and Merlin: Telling the Client's Story Using the Characters and Paradigm of the Archetypical Hero's Journey. *Seattle University Law Review* 29, no. 4: 767–803.

Ryömä, Arto. 2020. The Interplay of Heroic and Post-heroic Leadership: Exploring Tensions in Leadership Manifestations in the Oscillations between Onstage and Offstage Contexts. *Scandinavian Journal of Management* 36, no. 1: 1–15.

Singh, Sangeeta and Sonnenburg, Stephan. 2012. Brand Performances in Social Media. *Journal of Interactive Marketing* 26, no. 4: 189–197.

Tolkien, John R. R. 2004. *The Lord of the Rings*. London: HarperCollins.

Turner, Victor. 1969. *The Ritual Process: Structure and Antistructure*. New Brunswick: Aldine Transaction.

Van Gennep, Arnold. 1960. *The Rites of Passage*. London: Routledge.

Vogler, Christopher. 2007. *The Writer's Journey: Mythic Structure for Writers (3rd Edition)*. Studio City: Michael Wiese Productions.

Zimmer, Heinrich R. 1992. *Myths and Symbols in Indian Art and Civilization*. Edited by Joseph Campbell (8th Edition). Princeton: Princeton University Press.

Chapter 3

HYBRID HEROES IN EXTREMIS AND AT WORK

By Greg Stone

"You can't separate the rogue part from the heroes. They're just different sides of the bread."

Brian Hamilton, Philanthropist

"I wasn't so much arrested, as rescued."

John Christian, Bank robber-turned-CEO

Not so long ago, before the age of Trump, Professor Gautam Mukunda's mentor asked him why so many crazy people run countries (Mukunda 2012). The answer gave rise to a brilliant book called *Indispensable*. I will have much more to say about that later. In the meantime, we are exploring a new field of research called "heroism science," a term apparently coined three years after Mukunda's book appeared (Allison 1, 2015). Much of the scholarship in this area has been gloomy. For instance, psychologists Paul Babiak and Robert Hare produced startling statistics about mental illness in the executive suite in their book *Snakes in Suits*. They found that 3.5 percent of the 200 executives they studied were psychopaths, compared to just 1 percent of the general population (Babiak 2006). As if that statistic weren't scary enough, they argue that psychopathy, narcissism, and Machiavellianism form a "dark triad" in the corporate world. Unfortunately, many compromised leaders have ample charisma, which intensifies their impact and perhaps hides their faults (Mukunda 2012).

In this book, we have approached the hero (and her or his journey) from a hybrid perspective, on a spectrum from scoundrel to saint, with a dynamic outlook. We regard heroism not just as a personal characteristic, but as a series of actions in given situations and contexts. This is what makes "hybrid heroism" so fascinating, part of a tradition harking back to the story of Lucifer, the lapsed angel turned avenger. Instead of alternating between good and evil, the hybrid hero moves along a continuum between the extremes.

Storytellers have long understood the vast appeal of these warring opposites. Alfred Hitchcock believed that strong villains made strong movies (Stone 2019). Indeed, rogues and heroes often compose "opposing sides of the same story" (Gölz 2019, 27). In fact, we as audiences can experience fear and pleasure simultaneously, a phenomenon known as "co-activation," which explains the seemingly inexplicable appeal of horror (Stone 2019). Even mass marketer Disney exploits these contradictory sensations: witness the company's public relations campaign in Japan with the slogan "Welcome to the world of delightful villains" (Prusa 2016, 2). And speaking of colorful villains and their appeal, I interviewed entrepreneurs who made their way from prison to the executive suite, and in some cases, vice versa. Let's begin with a well-known rogue who never ran afoul of the law, though he certainly ran roughshod over any notions of benign management and common consideration.

Steve Jobs and His Chief Imitator

Walter Isaacson's excellent biography of the late Apple co-founder Steve Jobs details both his astounding achievements and his abject cruelty in ample detail. The list of Jobs' inventions is impressive beyond words: the Apple II computer, the Macintosh, the iPod, the iPhone, the App Store, the iPad, and iCloud. Moreover, he upended and revamped music distribution through iTunes and revolutionized the retail experience for hi-tech products through Apple Stores (Isaacson 2011)—creating, as Larry Ellison said, "the only lifestyle brand in the tech industry" (quoted in Isaacson 2011, 332). And oh, by the way, while serving as CEO of Pixar (at the same time he was running Apple), Jobs helped develop blockbusters like *Toy Story* and *Finding Nemo*. He was hailed as a "magician genius" who famously sneered at market research:

> Some people say, "Give the customers what they want". But that's not my approach. Our job is to figure out what they're going to want before they do. People don't know what they want until you show it to them. (Isaacson 2011, 567)

So much for his vaunted creativity and brilliance. To say that the obverse side of his personality was vicious would be an understatement. When I read Isaacson's biography, I was astounded by each description of Jobs' boorish and cruel behavior, only to discover a similar or worse example a few pages later, and so on and so on through nearly 600 pages. His personal habits were just as repellent as his behavior. When he worked at Atari for $5 an hour back in 1974, long before the PC revolution, he had such strong body odor and such a bad attitude that the company put him on the night shift. He'd even soak his feet in the toilet to calm himself down, a habit that disgusted his coworkers (Isaacson 2011). He was brash, blunt, and bombastic.

His callousness extended into his personal life too. When his on-again, off-again girlfriend, Chrisann Brennan, announced that she was pregnant, he refused to acknowledge paternity. After a paternity test established that the baby girl was, in fact his, Jobs still questioned the results. Later, he relented, though he often treated the child, whom they named Lisa, indifferently (Isaacson 2011). "On one visit he would be playful; on the next, he would be cold; often he was not there at all" (Isaacson 2011, 261).

One of Jobs' ex-girlfriends said he was a classic narcissist: "Expecting him to be nicer or less self-centered was like expecting a blind man to see," she said. "I think the issue is empathy—the capacity for empathy is lacking" (266). Though Jobs had a more stable home life when he later married Laurene Powell and fathered three more children, a boy and then two girls, he was never an attentive family man.

His behavior was especially irascible at Apple. The staff feared his vicious temper and mercurial ways. He perfected the technique of staring without blinking, which was quite disconcerting. John Sculley, who served as Apple's CEO, said his gaze was "unyielding, like an X-ray boring inside your bones, down to where you're soft and destructibly mortal" (206). Jobs had a binary view of people, who were either "enlightened" or assholes, and their work was "either 'the best' or 'totally shitty'" (119). Moreover, he might reverse his characterizations at a moment's notice. Colleagues described his allergy to the truth, often resulting in what they called a "reality distortion field": "If you tell him a new idea, he'll usually tell you he thinks it's stupid. But then, if he actually likes it, exactly one week later, he'll come back to you and propose your idea to you, as if he thought of it" (120).

Jobs often bullied his staff, though he justified his cruelty on the grounds that he had no tolerance for inferior work. He admitted at one gathering that he could be "a little hard to get along with" (a vast understatement), but he told the staff that they would send a "giant ripple through the universe" (143). One Apple executive called his method "management by character assassination" (196), yet he was able to elicit performance that coworkers never believed they could deliver. One might have expected that his struggles with pancreatic cancer would have caused him to reevaluate and temper his behavior, yet that was not the case. When he returned to work after a leave of absence, he savaged people he had not seen for six months and later said he was overjoyed to feel so creative. Indeed. His family hoped he'd be more attentive to them during his illness, but he still ignored them.

Though many might consider Jobs to be sui generis in his management style, he found a posthumous imitator in Elizabeth Holmes, of Theranos infamy, who modeled herself on him with disastrous results. This was a classic example of "imitatio heroica" (von den Hoff et al. 2015, 79). John Carreyrou captured Holmes' story in all its lurid fraudulence brilliantly in his book *Bad Blood*. For starters, Holmes copied Jobs's disarming habit of staring without blinking. She called her company's blood testing device, which allegedly produced rapid results, the "iPod of health care" (Carreyrou 2020, 30), she drove a car with no license plate, as Jobs did, and she also enveloped herself in a "reality distortion field that forced people to momentarily suspend disbelief" (291). Moreover, she affected a deep baritone to add to her ersatz gravitas. She would move from charm to hostility in an instant (8) to squash dissension, and she maintained an aura of brilliance that fooled many people who should have known better. Even though she dropped out of Stanford at age 19, one of her former professors said she was "a once-in-a-generation genius [like] Newton, Einstein, Mozart and Leonardo da Vinci" (280).

Eventually, Holmes fell like Icarus. In 2014, she was ranked 110 on the Forbes 400 with a net worth of $4.5 billion. By 2016, she was reduced to a footnote, with a net worth of zero (Kroll 2016). She was sentenced to 11 years in federal prison (with a possible reduction of two years for good behavior) for defrauding investors of hundreds of millions of dollars, though she has appealed the verdict. Needless to say, her company imploded. All in all, this was a spectacular failure that is a cautionary tale about hybrid heroism spilling over into villainy.

Progeny of Machiavelli: Effective Bullying?

Holmes' and Jobs' tales point directly toward the many paradoxes inherent in management, where the pursuit of seemingly inconsistent goals is an integral part of the job (Stone 2016). The leader must simultaneously execute and innovate, take responsibility for her own work and that of others, develop employees and evaluate them coldly, focus on today and plan for tomorrow, and, most relevant for this book, sometimes do harm to promote greater good. If we trace these ideas back many centuries to the source, we arrive at the philosophy of calculated ruthlessness put forth by Niccolò Machiavelli, whose book *The Prince* could serve as a blueprint for those seeking to rule or conquer through intimidation and to inflict injury when necessary (Machiavelli 2017). Carried through to a pitiless conclusion, this line of argument ends with his infamous observation that it is better to be feared than loved.

Machiavelli's advice may seem stark and callous to modern minds, possibly because of widespread belief in the "just-world hypothesis," that is, the notion that good people are compensated and bad people punished (Pfeffer 2010, 10). Jeffery Pfeffer from the Graduate School of Business at Stanford suggests that relinquishing the notion that life is fair will make leaders more vigilant. He argues that cultivating power is the key to success and notes that it is "20 percent given, 80 percent taken" (130). Moreover, Pfeffer explains how power both enhances and degrades those who possess it. On the one hand, it's linked to greater health and longevity, yet it makes leaders insensitive and causes "a tendency to see other people as a means to the power holder's gratification" (200). Unfortunately, Pfeffer claims, these drives are addictive. Other scholars have noted similar findings: "Power itself has profound, and usually toxic, effects […] [It] tends to make those who have it more sociopathic" (Mukunda 2013).

This often leads to unbridled anger. Unfortunately, studies have shown that venting wrath can be effective because it creates an impression of dominance, strength, competence, and intelligence (Pfeffer 2010). Political scientist Joseph Nye cites the example of 6′4″ Lyndon Johnson who "would physically get up front and personal, draping an arm around shorter men, and seizing others by their lapels and argu[ing] while pressing his face close to theirs" (Nye 2010, 325). Another case in point: Soichiro Honda (founder of the auto company that bears his name) was known to throw tools at incompetent workers (Pfeffer 2010)! A less harmful aspect of intimidation is merely looking the part: General Patton practiced scowling in the mirror and former President Trump wanted to look dour with a "tough-guy sourpuss" like Churchill (Thrush 2017). Yes, sad to say, bullying sometimes works because most people tend to avoid conflict (Pfeffer 2010).

Lest you misunderstand, we recognize that abject rudeness and naked aggression may have their place in leadership, but we are not advocating them. We are merely demonstrating that many executives resort to belligerence as a technique—becoming, in a sense, visionary bullies (Nye 2010). Yet unbridled overconfidence can certainly be disastrous. For instance, there is evidence that executives are boldest in rendering decisions on matters where they have little knowledge (Useem 2010, 512–513). F. Scott Fitzgerald illustrated this sort of "blind faith" in his novel *The Love of the Last Tycoon*, based on Irving Thalberg, a "boy wonder" who became head of production at Universal at age 20. Fitzgerald spent several years as a screenwriter in Hollywood and came to know Thalberg personally, as he explains in a revealing anecdote about feigned certainty:

> [Thalberg] said, "Scottie, supposing there's got to be a road through a mountain […] You say, 'Well, I think we will put the road there' and you trace it with your finger […] but you're the only one person that

knows that you don't know why you're doing it [...] [T]he people under you mustn't ever know or guess that you're in any doubt because they've all got to have something to look up to and they mustn't ever dream that you're in doubt about any decision." (Fitzgerald 1993, viii)

It is fair to say that leaders, whether as tough as Jobs or as mellow as Gandhi, are primarily concerned with the use, misuse, and possibly abuse of power. Power comes in many forms, however, and the categories are directly relevant to the concept of hybridity: Nye says that soft power calls for leadership through attraction, force of personality, communication, charisma, persuasion, rhetoric, or example, whereas hard power entails threats, inducements, intimidation, payments, rewards, hiring, firing, demotion, promotion, and compensation (Nye 2010, 315). The people you are about to meet might agree with Nye's concept of combining hard and soft power into something he calls "smart power" (305) for maximum effect.

Prison to Prosperity

Now let's look at a more extreme form of hybrid heroism, namely convicts-turned-CEOs and the benefactors who helped them. I had occasion to interview these intriguing people and I am sure that their stories will shed new light on the conflicting traits that successful executives often display (see Table 3.1).

Let's start with a program called *Inmates to Entrepreneurs*, under the auspices of the Brian Hamilton Foundation. Brian holds an MBA from Duke University and another degree in street life from his early childhood in a tough part of a Northeastern town. He jokes that the people from his neighborhood are either dead, in prison, or so rich that they own their own islands. Brian said his family "just didn't have any money at all" (Hamilton 2020,

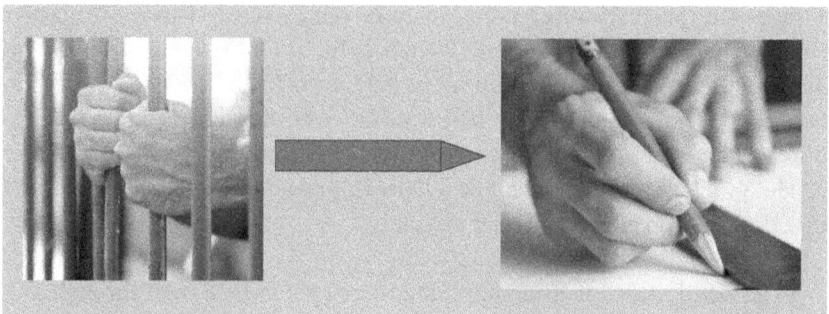

Figure 3.1 Risen from prison. Graphic by Greg Stone, photos from Shutterstock.

Table 3.1 Stories of hybrid heroes who are former convicts.

Lawrence Carpenter, convict-turned-owner of a commercial janitorial company
Scott Jennings, drug dealer-turned-owner of a fitness equipment installation company
John Christian, "Harvard Bank Robber"-turned-CEO of a behavioral health services
  firm
Tracy Mackness, drug dealer-turned-pig farmer
Daniel Manville, murderer-turned-law professor

Interview). They were on food stamps for a time because of huge medical bills for his handicapped sister. He says poverty means "not having anybody to guide you," yet he is a survivor: "I'm like a cockroach, you pile gasoline on me or whatever and I'll be crawling out of it the next day" (Interview).

An experienced entrepreneur who sold his own financial software company for a considerable sum, Brian has used his skills to help convicts. It all came about rather fortuitously. Though he has never been in jail himself, he and a friend who is a minister started working with prisoners some 30 years ago. Recognizing that it would be very difficult for convicts to find a job after their release, Brian had a eureka moment: They should "go and create one." Thus, an organization called Inmates to Entrepreneurs was born. It's now a national non-profit, supported by Brian's foundation.

All told, Brian has offered entrepreneurship courses to over 10,000 people formerly in prison. Astoundingly, 10–20 percent of them have started businesses! When I asked him for his views on hybrid heroism, Brian noted that inmates readily understand the unforgiving commercial world. He summed it up this way: "You have three people and two cookies" to divide. In his view, "you can't separate the rogue part from the heroes. They're just different sides of the bread" (Interview 2020).

One of Brian's success stories is that of former convict Lawrence Carpenter, who started selling drugs when he was 11 or 12 years old in Durham, North Carolina. He describes his younger self as a "street guy who was the worst of the worst," someone to be simply "counted out" (Carpenter 2020, Interview). At age 17, he landed in jail and spent six years there, followed by a second trip that ended in his late 20s. When he finally emerged, he realized that he wasn't cut out for college and that many jobs would be closed to him, so "I created my own market" (Interview). He started a cleaning service that began with residential customers, then graduated to commercial clients. The business now boasts 63 employees.

"You either roll over and quit," he says, "or you brush yourself off and keep fighting." Lawrence says he was always intelligent but had to learn to leave street slang behind and speak in a polished, professional style, and he also upgraded his appearance along with his conversational style. Now, "no one questions who I am," he said. He has lost only one contract because of his record. When he advises inmates, he implores them *not* to use their own names when they start a company (his firm is called SuperClean Professional Janitorial Services) so that their personal identities will be Google-proof, or at least harder to unearth. He says that many convicts flout this advice and end up failing because prospective customers can quickly find their police records online.

Scott Jennings is another one of the proud "graduates" of the Inmates to Entrepreneurs program. He describes himself as "the kid in 8th grade who bought candy for 10 cents and sold it for 25" (Jennings 2020, Interview). He got high for the first time at age 15, starting with pot, then occasionally psychedelics, and later began peddling ecstasy allegedly in tandem with a roommate whom he describes as his "toxic twin." Scott discovered that he had a natural talent for selling drugs, first pot, and eventually cocaine. "Drugs have always been a vehicle for my entrepreneurial spirit," he says. His own habit came to a screeching halt when he was arrested in his thirties. "Getting busted really ruined the buzz for about a year while I was waiting to be sentenced." He spent three years in prison and has now been sober for 16 years. (Jennings, Interview).

When he was released, he realized that his income would plummet down to $9 an hour, so he started a company called FitTech & Assembly (now SERVICERX)—first installing fitness machines in homes, then in businesses. He began with "75 dollars, an old pickup truck, a bag of tools and a lot of desperation" (Jennings, Interview). He had been so successful that he was contemplating taking a long vacation with a one-way ticket to Panama to become a landlord specializing in short-term rentals for travel businesses. Unfortunately, the pandemic destroyed that dream. He closed the rental business and dived back into the fitness equipment firm, which is now franchised. He explains his journey this way: "Jail was the driving force for what I didn't want to be. […] [My mother] didn't raise me to go to prison. I never want to be that person again" (Jennings, Interview).

How would he define hybrid heroism? He says he's a rebel with a "screwyou mentality." Yet he has come to realize that running a business does not mean challenging everybody. "It's our job to create wealth for ourselves and others in the process. It's not just about me anymore" (Jennings, Interview).

The "Harvard Bank robber"

John Christian is one of the most colorful executives that I have ever encountered. He grew up in a blue-collar suburb on the South Shore of Boston as the youngest of four children. Always a risk-taker and a renegade, by his own admission, he developed an alcohol problem starting in high school. Yet his hard-partying ways did not prevent him from gaining admission to Harvard, where he earned a degree in economics, with honors no less. Christian says he smoked pot nearly every day in college, then graduated to cocaine—all the while hiding his addictions from friends and family. On the surface, he was a model student. Thanks to his 6'2" muscular frame, he was also a member of the football team and even took boxing classes in the inner city. After college, he became a real estate developer and enjoyed great success until the recession of the early 1990s brought his empire crashing down. In the end, he stood on the front yard of his last property after it was foreclosed and realized that he had literally lost everything.

In desperate need of cash, he turned to robbing banks. At first, it was surprisingly easy. He remembers robbing a bank in the heart of Boston's posh Beacon Hill neighborhood and running down the street with a packet of cash that was spewing smoke after the booby-trap triggered. No one even gave him a second look. Another time, he emerged from a bank to discover a policeman on the street. He panicked, thinking that it was all over, but quickly realized that the cop was merely dropping his clothes off at a laundromat next door!

Christian's crime spree eventually reached a fever pitch. Over a nine-month period, he robbed 20 banks, netting just under $250,000 in cash, which he mostly used to fund a cocaine habit that reached the astronomical level of five to six grams a day. "I was literally led around by my nose," he jokes (Christian 2020, Interview). When he emerged from the bank where he committed his final robbery—the 21st in a long list—the FBI arrested him. The authorities had been trailing him for some time, and they waited until they could catch him in the act. "What took you so long?" he asked as he lay face down with his arms handcuffed behind his back (Christian, Interview).

Eight and a half years of prison followed, ending in 2000. For Christian, it was a time of growth and readjustment. He underwent a painful detox in a jail cell, started Alcoholics Anonymous chapters in two prisons, and trained for six years as a substance abuse counselor. Given that inmates tend to trust one of their own, he was able to communicate with fellow convicts in a way that officials could not. Moreover, prisoners tend to revere bank robbers for their daring and courage. As a result, he was, in many respects, at the top of the social ladder.

Never one to shirk responsibility, John admits that cocaine may have impaired his judgment and does not try to excuse his behavior. "Not every addict robs banks," he says. He thought he was above the law, or at least that it didn't apply to him. "Getting arrested was the greatest thing that happened to me," he says. "I wasn't so much arrested, as rescued. I joke that I'm allergic to alcohol and drugs now because they make me break out in handcuffs and fist fights" (Christian, Interview). He has been completely sober since July 15, 1991, a date he recites with proud specificity.

After his release, John worked as a counselor for homeless services for the city of Boston for 11 years, then became the CEO of Modern Assistance Programs, a company with 40 employees that supplies behavioral health services for 100,000 people, mostly members of trade unions. He recently opened Bridge Street Recovery, a 40-bed residential substance abuse and mental health facility in New Hampshire. He has also earned two master's degrees in psychology, one from the University of Western Alabama and another from Harvard. He says he got a lot more out of his Harvard education the second time around because "I wasn't smoking weed every day" (Christian, Interview). He also guest lectures every January in a course on persuasion at Harvard's Kennedy School and serves as an adjunct professor at the University of Massachusetts in Boston. Quite a turnaround in his fortunes.

Christian's take on hybrid heroism? He says his police record never goes away, nor does he shirk it. In fact, he refuses to seal it because it's part of who he is. Though he is not a psychopath, he believes that many company presidents would fit that description in that they have to make difficult decisions every day. He recalls working in his prior life in the cutthroat realm of real estate development, where brutality was common. He says there is a fine line between good and evil in all business endeavors, even in substance abuse counseling, where two deserving patients might vie for one bed. Deciding how to proceed requires a form of ruthlessness. Christian calls to mind a classic thought experiment in ethics: The brakes fail in a trolley car, and it hurtles toward five pedestrians on the track. The driver can switch to a different track, where only one person is standing, or leave matters alone and mow down five people. John says most executives would opt for the first choice, whereas many more cautious people might leave the resolution to chance or to God.

He says he has learned to control his confrontational nature. "Just because my first reaction might be to get angry and engage, doesn't mean I have to do that. I stop and listen to my second thought, not my first" (Christian, Interview). Age and experience help. At 67, he's measured. "Yet I can feel myself about to stray sometimes, and I am aware of where an explosion might take me." In many ways, his family is an anchor. He is married to a psychologist and has two stepchildren and two step-grandchildren. Domestic contentment, coupled with his impressive business success, have created a redemption narrative whose power drives him every day. He was also a party to a suit challenging discrimination in hiring in the public service sector in Massachusetts based on prior police records, and he points with pride and amusement to a wry reference from the progressive judge's decision, ruling in favor of the plaintiffs. The judge noted that he doubted that Moses would have been deemed an "unacceptable risk" as a leader of the Israelites because, so the Bible says, he had killed one of the Pharaoh's taskmasters when he saw him beating an enslaved worker (Cronin Case 2001).

Living in the fast lane, not the slow one

Tracy Mackness has a similar story, recounted in brutal honesty in her book *Jail Bird—The Life and Crimes of an Essex Bad Girl*. I found her to be as starkly frank as John Christian. Tracy says she has always been a "bad girl" and a rebel who shunned anything conventional (Mackness 2020, Interview). She attributes this partly to her dad, whom she revered as a hero, even though he was in and out of prison. As a teenager growing up outside of London, she developed an appetite for cocaine, speed, and ecstasy but never marijuana, which she found dulling. "I wanted to live in the fast lane, not the slow one," she jokes. Before long, she was stealing from stores—hiding high-ticket items like upscale faucets, gardening tools, and Black & Decker appliances in the bottom of shopping carts—then returning them the next day for refunds. She also learned the art of "kiting," buying credit cards stolen from unattended handbags or unlocked cars. She and her friends would practice the signatures and buy expensive goods, being careful not to exceed the credit limits. "We lived like poor millionaires," she says.

Tracy readily admits that she had bad taste in men. Companions with ordinary jobs bored her, so she would lose interest after a few days. She gravitated toward older men, especially bank robbers or gangsters. "I need stimulation at all times," she says. Her acquisitive nature kept her involved in crime because she has "champagne tastes on a beer budget." She liked fancy handbags and shoes and crazy weekends. She and her companions would routinely take drugs and party from Friday afternoon to Sunday without sleep or interruption. Come Monday, she would return to work at whatever conventional job she held at the time. The insanity came to a halt when she was sentenced at age 30 for 4 years. She spent two years in jail, only to return at age 37 for another seven and a half years after a three-month trial, which ended in a conviction for conspiracy to import a ton of cannabis.

That trial was harrowing beyond words. Tracy lost almost 50 pounds, to the point that her pants were constantly falling off. Unfortunately, prison was not her only experience in lockup. After a suicide attempt, she spent two months in a mental institution, where she was diagnosed with psychosis. A second trip to that institution followed, after a breakdown caused by depression and manic attacks. "I was so far gone that I thought there'd never be a point of return," she laments.

Yet return she did. In a prison work program, she discovered that she had a passion and a knack for pig farming, of all things. It happened suddenly when she looked into the sad, expressive eyes of a sow. "And something just clicked. There was a connection there. I felt a bit choked up, for her and for me" (Mackness, Jail Bird, 214). Fast forward to the present. At 58, she now runs her firm called Giggly Pigg Company. When she started in 2007, she had 30 pigs, surging to 800, but down to 400 since COVID-19. She sells her wares at 25 farmers' markets in Essex, makes 30 flavors of sausage (ranging from lemon/fennel to hickory smoked to caramelized onion), and employs eight people full-time and eight part-time.

Tracy says she's always been a manipulator. "I have the ability to make people see my point of view, and if they don't, I'll swing them around," she says. "I tend to get anything I want" (Mackness, Interview). Has her criminal background helped in business? "I was always a businesswoman. When I sold cocaine, I wanted to sell the best and sell the most. I was never a street dealer. I was an *importer*." She would smuggle in as much as 20 kilograms of cocaine at a time from other countries. Tracy says she's always been the "only woman in a man's world," (Mackness, Interview), both in the drug trade and in farming, so she has to make tough decisions.

When she speaks to convicts, she tells them, "I was once where you are. Look at what I've achieved in business. If I can do it, anyone can." She says she's a firm, but not a nasty manager. "Some say I'm horrible, but I see myself as direct. I tell employees that it's going to be my way. You'll be fine, as long as you do the right thing." Tracy says she's never violent, just formidable. "When you meet me, you know I won't take nonsense from man, woman, or beast," she says. Regrets? Though she attained high marks at school, she had a spotty attendance record. "I'm sorry I didn't study harder. Who knows? Maybe I could have been a lawyer or a member of parliament?" At the moment, she is content to be sedate. "I don't party any longer because it takes me a week to recover from what I used to do for a week" (Mackness, Interview).

Once an outlaw, now a law professor

We conclude the portraits of ex-convicts who transformed their lives with Daniel Manville, whose odyssey was perhaps the most dramatic of all. Along with three brothers and two sisters, Dan began his childhood in a rural area in Michigan's Upper Peninsula, then the family moved down to Ionia near Grand Rapids in the Lower Peninsula. After high school, he worked on the assembly line at Fisher Auto Body in Flint but found the job so dull that he enlisted in the army in 1966. Connections in the Pentagon helped keep him out of Vietnam and land a supposedly safer post on the border between

North and South Korea. Never one to turn down an adventure, Dan and a few friends went deer hunting in the demilitarized zone, a strip of unspoiled land that is 2.5 miles wide and 160 miles long. They were surrounded and almost killed when American forces mistook them for invaders. The next day, when four soldiers were killed, Dan realized that soldiering wasn't just a game (Manville 2020, Interview).

He returned to the US in 1968 and enrolled at Central Michigan University in Mount Pleasant where he maintained a 3.0 average, even though he was partying with abandon. As his political consciousness and anti-war sentiments developed, he channeled his frustrations into using and dealing drugs, including heroin, cocaine, mescaline, acid and "a lot of speed." He was mainlining and out of control. By 1972, "things fell apart" and his life took a dark turn as he crafted a macho image. He had become adept at karate in the army and was able to break bricks with his hands or his forehead. That aura of menace was complemented by a 32-caliber pistol that he carried in a shoulder holster. He made sure everyone was aware that he was armed.

When there was a break-in at a friend's apartment—where a large quantity of cocaine and money was stolen—Dan was the clear choice to teach the robber a lesson. The culprit, Terry, was easy to identify because he was flaunting sudden wealth. As Dan, his brother, and a third companion were driving in a snowstorm to Terry's apartment some 70 miles way in Mount Pleasant, their Ford Comet broke down. "We should have taken that as a sign," Dan said (Manville, Interview). With his experience with cars, he was able to repair the vehicle so they could keep going. When they arrived, Dan called the suspected thief (whom he knew) and told him he wanted to buy drugs, just as a ruse. Dan was immediately invited over to a basement apartment Terry shared with two others.

When they arrived, the swashbuckling trio of avengers drew guns and asked for the money and the cocaine back. Terry refused, so they tied him up. "I'm not proud of this," Dan said, "but I pistol-whipped him and stuck the barrel of my gun in his mouth" (Manville, Interview). Meanwhile, they tied up the other two young men as well. Dan and his accomplices happened to have chloroform on hand since one of them had stolen it from a chemistry lab at a community college he was attending. He generally used it as an intoxicant, but that day it became a knock-out drug. The trio gagged the bound men with rags infused with the anesthetic. Then they absconded with the drugs, left the apartment, shot up the drugs, and proceeded to have a party.

The next day, they found out that Terry had died from the chloroform. Since this was the first murder in Mount Pleasant in 22 years, the police went on a rampage and started questioning "every hippie in sight." Dan was a likely suspect because "I looked like Charlie Manson." He thought about going on the run but decided to stay put. A month later, he was arrested and charged with first-degree murder, felony murder, second-degree murder, and armed robbery.

Facing a possible sentence of life without parole, he pleaded guilty after much negotiation and was freed on bond. He did so much speed while awaiting sentencing that he developed an abscess in one of his lungs. Yet reality awaited him. His sentence was 4.5–15 years.

When Dan arrived at Jackson Prison, his brother was already in custody and had wrangled a job for him as an intake worker who assisted with new arrivals. His brother bribed someone with two cartons of cigarettes so that Dan was initially housed in the prison hospital, where he spent the next 72 days recovering from his lung ailment. When he eventually moved into a cell, he immediately fell back into dealing drugs—relying on guards who smuggled in contraband to supplement their meager income. At the same time, he earned college degrees and started studying law on his own. The academic work allowed him to create the illusion that he had a life apart from his day-to-day existence as a "caged animal," who was just marking time until the end of his sentence.

Dan thought he was a master manipulator, but after the parole board denied his request for early release, he sat down in his cell and asked himself what he wanted to do with the rest of his life. The choices were: "one, continuing to deal drugs, which meant I'd end up killing again or being killed, two dealing drugs in a college environment, but I was too old, or three becoming a lawyer, judge, or legislator." A career as a lawyer seemed to be the best option. Planning ahead, he took the Law School Admissions Test while he was behind bars.

For the most part, fellow inmates left him alone because he had a reputation as a "hit man." When confronted, he'd simply say, "Either jump me or fuck off," and most people backed down. In one memorable confrontation, he doused three rivals with lighter fluid (in the 1970s, inmates were allowed to have cigarette lighters) and threatened to set them on fire. Point made. Eventually, Dan became a trustee and was paroled in 1976, after serving "three years, four months, 20 days, 22 hours, and 17 minutes," a phrase he rattles off with palpable relief. Yet leaving was traumatic. He was terrified on his first day of freedom because prison had been "like a womb," where all his needs were satisfied. He had "a bed, food and structure all around. I was simply a number: 135706. I felt as if it was tattooed onto my forehead" (Manville, Interview). He moved forward, though, enrolling in a paralegal program, and also earning a master's degree in criminal justice from Michigan State University. After he was admitted to law school at Antioch in Washington, D.C., he returned to drug dealing ("In those days you could get an ounce of cocaine delivered by FedEx," he said). As graduation approached, however, he shaved his beard, cut his hair, and decided to change the trajectory of his life. That was only the first hurdle. It took him five years and several court hearings before he convinced the Michigan Bar Association to admit him to practice. A hard-won achievement.

He began his new career as a criminal lawyer, handling misdemeanor cases for offenders who knew him from his days in prison, then made a name for himself with prominent prisoners' rights cases in federal court. He became a go-to expert and, by the mid-80s, published the *Prisoner's Self-Help Litigation Manual*, now in its fourth edition, at a dictionary-size with 940 pages. Due to his expertise, he landed teaching positions in law schools, first at Wayne State University, then at the University of Denver, and finally at Michigan State University, where he is a clinical professor and the director of the Civil Rights Clinic. His students handle actual cases in federal courts, and he teaches them practical skills such as filing motions, conducting oral arguments, writing briefs, and questioning witnesses. That experience makes them stand out when they interview for jobs.

Is the wild man still lurking in Dan's personality? In some ways, yes, he admits, but he has learned to control his anger. "I get mad now, but I get over it. Plus, I'm in my 70s so I'm mellow," he says with a laugh. A group of good friends who took him into their families upon his release from prison have helped him stay relaxed, not to mention a woman who has been his life partner for almost 20 years. He confesses that he feels guilty about the murder, especially because "I'm still enjoying life after more than 50 years, and the victim has been in the ground all this time. I don't think I'll ever even the scale," he says. "I took a life. Not for god and country, as in the military, but for reasons that were simply selfish." As he explains, "My rebellion has continued since I left prison. Now I'm fighting to ensure that juries will hear the stories of convicts who are victims of an inhumane criminal justice system. Victories may be small, but they are sweet" (Manville, Interview). Even though he has been free for 47 years, he said prison never leaves his thoughts. He dreams about it at least a couple of times a month.

Fools to Revere

We turn now from former convicts to another form of hybrid heroism: the fool, be he or she holy, profane, benign, or destructive, often found not just in the literary realm but in the business world as well. Consultant David Firth compiled a list of the various corporate "fools" who challenge orthodoxy in constructive ways, including the alienator, the contrarian, the jester, the satirist and the truthseeker (Firth, The Corporate Fool). In Chapter 2, Stephan noted that fools are both despised and tolerated, degraded and privileged. Reviewing the vast number of these characters in world literature, we would have to agree. It does seem, however, that writers have been fascinated for millennia with the entertainment value of fools.

One of the first fictional fools is Thersites in *The Iliad*. Homer describes him as bowlegged and lame, with hunched shoulders—a rough-hewn creature despised by both Achilles and Odysseus (Homer 2011, 23). Worn out by nine hard years of fighting, Thersites taunted King Agamemnon and accused him of selfishness in an obscenely vituperative anti-war rant: "What more do you want? Your huts spill over with bronze and are stocked with women to serve you ... Do you want more gold ... or one more beautiful girl to screw in your hut" (Homer 2011, 24)?

Whereupon Odysseus struck him with his staff and reduced him to silence. Though he did not succeed in ending the war, the comical Thersites was nonetheless a compelling character who makes repeat appearances in literature and philosophy. In Plato's Republic, he shows up as a buffoon in the afterlife in the body of an ape (Plato 1961, 843; he is mentioned again in Sterne's *Tristram Shandy*, in Goethe's *Faust*, and even in Hegel's *Introduction to the Philosophy of History*.

Plato seems to be a great source for tales of the ridiculous. In *The Republic*, he tells a story about incompetent sailors fighting for control of a vessel. Sebastian Brant picked up this thread in 1494 in his satirical allegory *Ship of Fools*, where a group of ludicrous characters make their way to the fool's paradise of Narragonia, as memorialized in woodcuts by Albrecht Dürer (see Figure 3.2).

Figure 3.2 *Ship of Fools* by Albrecht Dürer (WikiCommons).

The *Ship of Fools* allegory has reemerged in twentieth-century art and literature, notably in Katherine Ann Porter's novel (of the same name, published in 1962) depicting a group of disillusioned expatriates sailing from Mexico to Germany before World War II, in the music of The Doors, Robert Plant, the Grateful Dead, and John Cale, not to mention a short story by none other than the Unabomber Ted Kaczynski! Perhaps readers or listeners who consider themselves enlightened feel some satisfaction as they congratulate themselves on their self-appointed superiority. We sometimes take comfort when we compare ourselves to those who flounder.

Other literary fools that come to mind are "innocents," like Prince Myshkin in *The Idiot*, Benji in *The Sound and the Fury*, Boo Radley in *To Kill a Mockingbird*, and Lenny in *Of Mice and Men*. Among the most colorful are a band of charming rogues led by a character named Mack in Steinbeck's *Cannery Row*. The rascals survive with odd jobs, minor scams, and jugs of wine, all the while spurning the society whose tolerance sustains them. A character called Doc is a learned scientist who admires their peculiar genius as he watches them ignore a parade that is passing by:

> There are your true philosophers […] In a time when people tear themselves to pieces with ambition […] they are relaxed. All of our so-called successful men [have] bad stomachs, and bad souls, but Mack and the boys […] can satisfy their appetites without calling them something else. (Steinbeck 2009, 9003)

This is a poignant expression of the detached wisdom of noble fools, comfortable in their indolence and indifferent to the trappings of success. In their poverty, they are rich with insight.

Perhaps no writer understood the appeal of fools better than Shakespeare. He was the master chronicler of folly in action—whose jesters achieved a whole new level of complexity and subtlety—with direct bearing on the concept of hybridity. Fools in his plays serve as sages, foils, irritants, and counselors to those in power. In *Henry IV Part 1*, for instance, the king rebukes his son Prince Harry for keeping company with miscreants like Sir John Falstaff, a drunkard, conniver, and whoremaster, who is nonetheless a knight. At the same time, the king recognizes Harry's dual nature, with "low desires" commingling with "the greatness of the blood" and "thy princely heart" (Henry IV Part 1, 83). The sly, grasping Falstaff crafts a close relationship with Harry that, for a time, benefits both. The prince gains amusement, and the corpulent companion reflected glory. "I am the fellow with the great belly, and he my dog," the roguish knight says (Henry IV Part 2, 16).

When Harry takes over the throne after his father's death and becomes King Henry V, he summarily rejects Falstaff and imprisons him, in effect amputating the irresponsible part of his own nature and recognizing that his relationship with the ne'er-do-well Sir John is more parasitic than symbiotic: "I have turned away my former self," Henry declares (Henry the Fourth, Part 2, 120).

Indeed, the Henry plays overflow with double imagery, showing the dual nature of heroes, encompassing virtue and sin. They are replete with verbal jiu-jitsu, with clashing images that yield insight. For instance, in a prescient soliloquy that predicted his future, Henry likens his metamorphosis to a sun breaking through poisonous clouds: "And like bright metal on a sullen ground,/My reformation, glittering o'er my faults, Shall grow more goodly" (Henry the Fourth, Part 1, 25). In the words of the Archbishop of Canterbury, Henry's evolution from rogue to statesman occurred when "Consideration like an angel came/And whipp'd th'offending Adam out of him" (Henry the Fifth, 4). In sum, Shakespeare has created in poetic form a portrait of the hybrid hero in Prince Harry/Henry V, with warring traits of malevolence and benevolence. In this sense, Shakespeare presages modern heroes—with complex though mutable dichotomous personalities—who transform themselves with bold, affirmative actions over the course of their development, as Inge suggested in Chapter 1.

The bard later achieved new heights of biting humor in the person of King Lear's fool, who serves as a binary antipode to his master. King and fool are linked, as one and zero, and the juxtaposition creates a dialectic between sagacity and idiocy that blurs into a synthesis. When, for instance, the aging, demented Lear declares that "nothing can be made of nothing," (Lear, 37), the fool later taunts him by observing, "I am a fool, thou art nothing" (39). He mocks Lear's lax parenting of his two unfaithful daughters in a series of witty epigrams:

> *Fool:* I can tell why a snail has a house.
> *Lear:* Why?
> *Fool:* Why, to put his head in; not to give it away to his daughters, and leave his horns without a case (46–47).
> *Fool:* [...] [T]hou mad'st thy daughters thy mothers, for thou gav'st them the rod and putt'st down thine own breeches (38).

The fool describes himself as "Lear's shadow" (40), the simpleton who assumes the mantle of the wise man, or the sycophant who sometimes acts like the dominant party. He bemoans the way truth and falsehood, accuracy and deception commingle in the king's topsy-turvy government: "Thou hast pared thy wit o' both sides, and left nothing i' th' middle" (38). If any courtier or duke had uttered these insults, he would have paid with his life, but the fool has special status that allows him to speak freely, for the king's benefit, if only he were prudent enough to listen. Because of his wit and the undeniable insights he offers, the fool can mock Lear from a position of safety and serve as the antipode to the king's even greater folly.

A Scale for Evaluating Leaders

At this stage in our analysis, we may wonder whether there is a mechanism that can help identify heroism or its opposite. The answer lies partly in Gautam Mukunda's superb book *Indispensable*, propounding "Leader Filtration Theory" (Mukunda 2012, 21), based on the premise that "the best and worst [leaders] can seem very similar, and that the processes that give you the best leaders are essentially the same as those that give you the worst ones" (219). Mukunda offers insights into "unfiltered" leaders at the extremes, far away from the more common "modal" types who rise up through the ranks. The outliers tend to have little or no experience, and they bypass the customary filtration process by dint of charisma or connections. They also exhibit a broad spectrum of psychological disorders, chiefly paranoia and narcissism (15), and they either achieve "great triumph [or] great disaster" (224). Though "modal" leaders may be perfect for ordinary circumstances (221), they may not be appropriate for exigent situations calling for greater creativity.

Mukunda analyzed the performance of all U.S. presidents (through George W. Bush) and determined that seven of the top ten were "unfiltered," including Lincoln, Franklin Delano Roosevelt, Washington, Theodore Roosevelt, and Wilson, while many of the bottom ten were in the same category, including Coolidge, Tyler, Grant, Andrew Johnson, and Harding (Mukunda 2012). Lincoln not only captured the top rating but also emerged as the prototypical unproven outlier, with no demonstrated political skills when he took office. He had served only one undistinguished term in Congress and later lost an election to the Senate. Moreover, his background was atypical: he was the first president who had not been born in the original 13 colonies and the first from a state west of the Appalachians (Mukunda 2012). Despite his unorthodox background and scant experience, however, Lincoln was certainly a genius, with a flair for writing and storytelling, and a driving ambition that was "like a little engine that knew no rest" (95). Unfortunately, he also suffered from the tragic flaw of mental illness that often plagues extreme leaders (Mukunda 2012). He had a lifelong history of depression that twice brought him to the threshold of suicide, and he suffered at least two breakdowns (Mukunda 2012). During the second bout, friends went so far as to remove razors and knives from his room!

Mukunda's book clearly shows us that great success is often accompanied by equally huge flaws. Many of the most effective leaders have suffered profoundly and experienced lucidity and confusion, exaltation and degradation, insight and stupidity, confidence and despair. They are truly hybrid in that they exhibit wildly contradictory traits that are somehow combined into an efficient machine. Pure saints are as rare as unadulterated villains.

References

Allison, Scott T. 2015. The Initiation of Heroism Science. *International Advances in Heroism Science* 1, no. 1: 1–9.

Babiak, Paul and Hare, Robert D. 2006. *Snakes in Suits: When Psychopaths Go to Work.* New York: HarperCollins.

Carpenter, Lawrence. January 20, 2020, updated, June 23, 2023. Owner SuperClean Professional Janitorial Services, Raleigh-Durham-Chapel Hill, NC. Interview by Author.

Carreyrou, John. 2020. *Bad Blood: Secrets and Lies in a Silicon Valley Startup.* New York: Vintage.

Christian, John. July 7, 2020, updated June 23, 2023. President & CEO, Modern Assistance, Quincy, MA. Interview by Author.

Cronin, V. O'Leary. August 14, 2001. Commonwealth of Massachusetts Superior Court No. 00-1713-F.

Firth, David. The Corporate Fool and the Search for Healthy Organisations. *Soulful Living.* https://www.soulfulliving.com/corporatefool.htm.

Fitzgerald, F. Scott. 1993. *The Love of the Last Tycoon.* New York: Scribner.

Gölz, Olmo. 2019. The Imaginary Field of the Heroic: On the Contention between Heroes, Martyrs, Victims and Villains in Collective Memory. *helden. heroes. héros.: E-Journal on Cultures of the Heroic*, special issue 5: 27–38.

Hamilton, Brian. January 28, 2020, updated June 23, 2023. Philanthropist, Brian Hamilton Foundation, Holly Springs, NC. Interview by Author.

Homer. *The Iliad.* 2011. Translated by Stephen Mitchell. New York: Free Press.

Isaacson, Walter. 2011. *Steve Jobs.* New York: Simon & Schuster.

Jennings, Scott. February 25, 2020, updated Jun 23, 2023. Owner, SERVICERX, Raleigh, NC. Interview by Author.

Kroll, Luisa, October 6, 2016. From Bad to Worse: Forbes 400's Biggest Drop-Off Elizabeth Holmes Announces More Grim News. *Forbes.* https://www.forbes.com/sites/luisakroll/2016/10/06/from-bad-to-worse-forbes-400s-biggest-drop-off-elizabeth-holmes-announces-more-grim-news/?sh=7304beb87b0c.

Machiavelli, Niccolò. 2017. *The Prince.* Translated by W. K. Marriott. Mineola: Dover.

Mackness, Tracy. July 9, 2020. Director, The Giggly Pig Company, Romford, England. Interview by Author.

Mackness, Tracy and Crewe, Deborah. 2013. *Jail Bird – The Life and Crimes of an Essex Bad Girl.* London: Simon & Schuster.

Manville, Daniel. July 10, 2020. Clinical Professor and Director of the Civil Rights Clinic at Michigan State University. Interview by Author.

Mark, Margaret and Pearson, Carol S. 2015. *The Hero and the Outlaw: Building Extraordinary Brands Through the Power of Archetypes.* New York: McGraw-Hill.

Mukunda, Gautam. 2012. *Indispensable: When Leaders Really Matter.* Boston: Harvard Business Review Press.

———. 2013. Don't Trust Anyone Over 70: Why old Leaders are Dangerous. 27 February. https://foreignpolicy.com/2013/02/27/dont-trust-anyone-over-70/.

Nye, Joseph H. 2010. Power and Leadership. In *Handbook of Leadership Theory and Practice*, edited by Nitin Nohria and Rakesh Khurana, 305–332. Boston: Harvard Business Press.

Pfeffer, Jeffery. 2010. *Power: Why Some People Have it – And Others Don't.* New York: HarperCollins.

Plato. *The Collected Dialogues.* 1961. Edited by Edith Hamilton and Huntington Cairns. Princeton: Princeton University Press.

Porter, Katherine Anne. 2015. *Ship of Fools.* New York: Open Road.

Prusa, Igor. 2016. Heroes Beyond Good and Evil: Theorising Transgressivity in Japanese and Western Fiction. *Electronic Journal of Contemporary Japanese Studies* 16, no. 1. http://www.japanesestudies.org.uk/ejcjs/vol16/iss1/prusa.html.

Shakespeare, William. 1954. *King Henry the Fourth Part I.* New Haven: Yale University Press.

———. 1955. *Henry the Fifth.* New Haven: Yale University Press.

———. 1956. *King Henry the Fourth Part II.* New Haven: Yale University Press.

———. 1956. *King Lear.* New Haven: Yale University Press.

Steinbeck, John. 2009. *The Short Novels of John Steinbeck.* New York: Penguin.

Stone, Greg. 2016. *Artful Business: 50 Lessons from Creative Geniuses.* Scotts Valley: Amazon CreateSpace.

———. 2019. *Branding with Powerful Stories: The Villain, Victims, and Heroes Model.* Santa Barbara: Praeger.

Thrush, Glenn and Haberman, Maggie. 2017. Why Letting Go, for Trump, is no Small or Simple Task. *The New York Times*, 21 March. https://www.nytimes.com/2017/03/21/us/politics/trump-obama-wiretapping-motivation.html.

Useem, Michael. 2010. Decision Making as Leadership Foundation. In *Handbook of Leadership Theory and Practice*, edited by Nitin Nohria and Rakesh Khurana, 507–525. Boston: Harvard Business Press.

Von den Hoff, Ralf, Schreurs-Morét, Anna, Posselt-Kuhli, Christina, Hubert, Hans W. and Heinzer, Felix. 2015. Imitatio Heroica: On the Impact of a Cultural Phenomenon. *helden. heroes. héros.: E-Journal on Cultures of the Heroic*, special issue 5: 79–95.

Chapter 4

THE MEANING OF HYBRID HEROES FOR INDIVIDUALS, BUSINESSES, AND SOCIETY: A CONCLUDING ROUND-TABLE DISCUSSION

What does the concept of hybrid heroes mean to people and businesses, and how do the notions differ in various cultures? How can we apply the theory, and what are the pitfalls? As we all come from different backgrounds, we discussed our perspectives.

How should we define the concept of hybrid heroes?

Inge: I would define a hybrid hero as someone who possesses heroic traits, performs heroic acts, or acts as a moral leader but engages *at the same time* in acts that can be considered criminal, villainous, or law-breaking. Hybrid heroes are not just flawed but conflicted with regard to their motivations and aspirations, and ultimately with who they are.
Greg: In my view, the hybrid hero has a dual nature, part saint and part scoundrel, moving along a spectrum. You might say that the warring traits in his or her personality are twins. They may be identical or fraternal, but they come from the same gene pool. As we have noted, research shows that an inclination to psychopathy is not uncommon in executive suites. We have also observed Machiavelli's pervasive influence on modern capitalism, and we have portrayed leaders who possessed traits at the extreme ends of the spectrum—including criminals who resurrected themselves as benevolent leaders. In sum, hybrid heroes display fascinating combinations of folly and wisdom and malevolence and benevolence.
Stephan: I totally agree with you guys. Hybrid heroines and heroes oscillate between saint and scoundrel. However, in the long run, the saint must prevail. If not, there is the big danger that a person or a team will drift into evil. Then the hybrid hero would become a total villain.

What does the concept of the hybrid hero mean for your area of expertise?

Greg: As an executive coach, I often advise clients to embrace dichotomous traits. After all, management requires great comfort with paradox. Leaders must be compassionate but tough, bold yet cooperative, ambitious yet humble. They need to guide their subordinates, but at the same time tolerate their divergent styles and eccentricities. As Nye suggests, they should combine soft power, that is, leadership through communication, charisma, or persuasion, with hard power, that entails threats, intimidation, or rewards (Nye 2010).

Stephan: The hybrid hero concept is quite conducive for learning, especially in the university where it can spur more creative educational approaches. Often, we expect students to follow an established set of guidelines. What a mistake! They should learn to deal with ambiguities, paradoxes, in-between worlds, and fields of tension instead. In my teaching, I try to encourage my students to follow their own paths and to avoid quick solutions.

Inge: I agree with Stephan that the concept of hybrid heroes can be a helpful instrument for learning in a variety of contexts, such as organizational life, career coaching and in university education. Hybrid heroes can add complexity to the learning process. Because of internet blogs and popular articles offering bromides on management, students often enter university assuming there will be a well-structured 10-step process of becoming a moral leader. Yet, real life is messy and complex and nobody is perfect. We tend to avoid looking at our personal pitfalls, our failures, and our inner demons, but facing up to them and daring to reflect on our own paradoxes and complexities can help us become more fully-rounded people.

What can we learn from hybrid heroes? What are opportunities this blended archetype can bring us?

Inge: Though this may seem counterintuitive, hybrid heroes can actually be useful archetypes—but *only* when we critically reflect on them. Traditional heroes are often considered to be exemplars of "good" behavior and are thereby put on a somewhat untouchable and distant pedestal. Of course, "saintlike" heroes can motivate and inspire moral decision-making. Yet, when we try to follow them and fail—which we likely will at some point—it's too easy to just give up. Hybrid heroes are an antidote for dichotomous thinking, such as "entirely good" versus "utterly bad." Reflecting on decisions and actions can enhance our capacity for moral complexity and help us explore our own moral ambiguities. Slipping up is part of life, and not a reason to relinquish our good intentions or shy away from moral reflection.

Greg: We can, perhaps, learn to accept our worst traits, and even embrace them, provided we stay on the near side of ethics and the law. Too often we are held to extreme and unrealistic notions of purity, in word and deed. History shows us, in no uncertain terms, that those we revere most were often deeply flawed. Why should we be different? There's an old saying that charity means forgiving others, and wisdom means forgiving yourself. When faced with a moral dilemma, we might consider a thought experiment where we contemplate the worst and most despicable course of action and work backward from that toward a more viable solution. Only through pitiless scrutiny can we arrive at true enlightenment. Please understand that I am not advocating cruelty or ruthlessness. I am merely suggesting that the best leaders need to evaluate every option.

Stephan: Simply put, a hybrid hero's understanding can bring more meaning, more variety, and more happiness to our lives.

What are the pitfalls and drawbacks of the hybrid hero?

Inge: As I mentioned before, reflection is a prerequisite for discovering the positive opportunities of hybrid heroes. *Without* reflection, however, I think problems could ensue. When people postpone moral judgment in order to enjoy a hybrid hero story, they may actually become attracted to the villainous traits of a hybrid hero. Thus, without reflection, our tendency for fast decision-making may lead us to consider villainy as admirable. As a thought experiment it may be entertaining to imagine yourself as a clever bank robber (like the characters of *La Casa de Papel*) or a murderous vigilante with a code (as in *Dexter Morgan*). Nonetheless, it could be problematic when you internalize these protagonists as praiseworthy. Copycat behavior—for example the real-life murderer who imitated the style of Dexter Morgan—is probably rare. However, confusing the villainous sides of the hybrid hero with exemplary behavior may have a more subtle impact on our norms, values and our aspirations. In our research on *The Wolf of Wall Street*, for instance, business students and sales professionals uncritically viewed Jordan Belfort—regardless of his corrupt behavior—as a winner, hero, and role model without much conscious reflection. Considering his conduct admirable might lead to the normalization of criminal behavior and clouding of moral judgment.

Greg: I agree with Inge that reflection is necessary in this context to help, for want of a better term, "deglamorize" villains, especially for the young and impressionable. As I explain in my book *Branding with Powerful Stories: The Villains, Victims, and Heroes Model*, scoundrels hold endless fascination. In many cases, their lives are more dramatic than those of law-abiding citizens. Would you rather read a biography of Bluebeard the pirate, or a selfless saint? As we study dictators from past (and present) times, we wonder why they kill with such reckless abandon. Do they do it just because they can, or do they have a hidden agenda? Historians estimate that Joseph Stalin murdered up to 20 million of his own people with no justification, while Chairman Mao may have terminated the lives of as many as 80 million through a combination of outright violence and engineered famines. What can we learn from these horrifying examples? We should bear in mind that Stalin began as a seminary student and wrote sensitive poetry in his youth. To be clear, I excuse *nothing* in the lives of these brutal autocrats. I merely suggest that students and leaders alike consider the full panoply of human behavior as we struggle with ethical issues.

Stephan: Heroism, whether hybrid or not, always carries the danger that others will aspire to copy the lives of heroes. But it's really about each individual on her or his own hybrid journey, with all the ups and downs. As Inge and Greg have already pointed out, reflection is the key, not only for a good balance between scoundrel and saint but also to forge one's own way, enriched by role models without copying them.

How do hybrid heroes shape other structures in societies, such as businesses, cultures and norms and values?

Stephan: Our understanding of hybrid heroes is not only helpful for individuals, teams, or organizations, but also in broadening our views of modern societies to explain cultures that are becoming more and more complex. In addition, our understanding can help counter the current tendency of radicals on the right and left of the political spectrum who merely offer simple solutions. There is no shortage of convincing ideas to address global challenges. However, most of them are overly simplistic. I see the storytelling potential of hybrid heroes, in particular the framework of the hybrid heroic journey, as a fruitful means of encouraging subtlety in reasoning.

Inge: I agree! Hybrid heroes can counteract people's longing for simplistic ideas and easy answers and can enhance our tolerance for ambiguity and help us grasp the complexity of organizations and society. Awareness of heroes-turned-villains can help people process traumas of the past, and current hybrid heroes can help people reflect on society today and find new paths for the future. If someone like Jordan Belfort is perceived by many as a hybrid hero, what does that say about our society and the role models we admire? Unlike people in marginalized parts of society, real-life hybrid heroes may easily get away with criminal behavior, as if their talent, success, wealth, or charm provides them with a "free pass" when it comes to harming others, acting selfishly, or twisting facts. The popularity of the hybrid hero perhaps reflects our ambivalent attitude toward this trend. We long for heroes and we are motivated to view them in a positive light. The concept of hybrid heroes allows us to simultaneously notice their villainous side.

Concluding Thoughts

In this book, we have explored hybrid heroes from various angles. We have reflected on the range, consequences, dangers, and opportunities of this new concept. While the journey of this book is over, we hope to spark critical reflection and awareness of this blended archetype. In the so-called "postheroic" world, there are still aspects of new models that require more research as we move beyond traditional concepts of heroes, with a potential focus on gender, power, or sex lenses (Fletcher 2004) and a new approach of "mutuality and more fluid power relations, where leadership practices [...] are distributed throughout the organization rather than located in a few at the top" (656). In many respects, heroism, in all its hybrid complexity, can permeate an entire corporate structure from the highest to the lowest levels. Indeed, focusing on the managerial suites as the principal locus of exemplary behavior is outmoded. Every employee and each citizen can serve as a role model on their journeys through work and life.

As we conclude this book, we invite you to think about the hybrid heroes you have encountered in your life and to join the debate. Perhaps Bobby Butcher in *The Boys* had a point when he said, "Heroes are just villains who get good press."

References

Fletcher, Joyce K. 2004. The Paradox of Postheroic Leadership: An Essay on Gender, Power, and Transformational Change. *The Leadership Quarterly* 15, no. 5: 624–661.

Nye, Joseph H. 2010. Power and Leadership. In *Handbook of Leadership Theory and Practice*, edited by Nitin Nohria and Rakesh Khurana, 305–332. Boston: Harvard Business Press.

INDEX

www.ingramcontent.com/pod-product-compliance
Lightning Source LLC
Chambersburg PA
CBHW031447280326

41927CB00037B/388